Paul Hannon

HILLSIDE

HILLSIDE GUIDES - ACROSS THE NORTH

Long Distance Walks
- •COAST TO COAST WALK   •CLEVELAND WAY COMPANION
- •WESTMORLAND WAY   •FURNESS WAY   •CUMBERLAND WAY
- •DALES WAY •LADY ANNE'S WAY   •NORTH BOWLAND TRAVERSE

Circular Walks - Lancashire
- •BOWLAND   •PENDLE & THE RIBBLE

Circular Walks - Yorkshire Dales
- •HOWGILL FELLS   •THREE PEAKS   •MALHAMDALE
- •WHARFEDALE   •NIDDERDALE   •WENSLEYDALE   •SWALEDALE

Circular Walks - North York Moors
- •WESTERN MOORS   •SOUTHERN MOORS   •NORTHERN MOORS

Circular Walks - South Pennines
- •BRONTE COUNTRY   •CALDERDALE   •ILKLEY MOOR

Circular Walks - Peak District
- •EASTERN PEAK   • NORTHERN PEAK   • CENTRAL PEAK
- • SOUTHERN PEAK   • WESTERN PEAK

Circular Walks - North Pennines
- •TEESDALE   •EDEN VALLEY

Hillwalking - Lake District
- •OVER LAKELAND MOUNTAINS   •OVER LAKELAND FELLS

Yorkshire Pub Walks
- •HARROGATE/WHARFE VALLEY   •HAWORTH/AIRE VALLEY

Large format colour hardback

FREEDOM OF THE DALES

BIKING COUNTRY
- •YORKSHIRE DALES CYCLE WAY   •WEST YORKSHIRE CYCLE WAY
- •MOUNTAIN BIKING - WEST & SOUTH YORKSHIRE
- •AIRE VALLEY BIKING GUIDE   •CALDERDALE BIKING GUIDE
- • GLASGOW Clyde Valley & Loch Lomond

- • YORK WALKS *City Theme Walks*

- •WALKING COUNTRY TRIVIA QUIZ *Over 1000 questions*

Send S.A.E. for up-to-date details and pricelist

WALKING COUNTRY

SOUTHERN PEAK

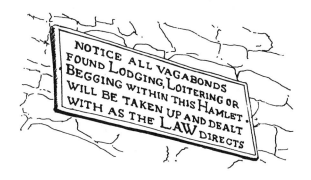

Paul Hannon

HILLSIDE

HILLSIDE
PUBLICATIONS
11 Nessfield Grove
Keighley
West Yorkshire
BD22 6NU

First published 1997

© Paul Hannon 1997

ISBN 1 870141 52 0

The author would like to acknowledge the assistance of Roland Smith, Head of Information Services at the Peak National Park, for his invaluable help in looking over the manuscript. Any errors, however, remain the author's.

Cover illustrations:
Wolfscote Dale; Robin Hood's Stride; Hartington
Back cover: Ilam Rock, Dovedale
(Paul Hannon/Big Country Picture Library)

Page 1: Harborough Rocks
Page 3: At Alport

Printed in Great Britain by
Carnmor Print and Design
95-97 London Road
Preston
Lancashire
PR1 4BA

CONTENTS

INTRODUCTION...6

THE WALKS *(mileage in brackets)*

INTRODUCTION

THE PEAK NATIONAL PARK

The Peak District was designated Britain's first National Park in 1951, and embracing an area of 555 square miles it is the most popular in the country. While commonly allotted to Derbyshire, substantial parts fall within Staffordshire, Yorkshire and Cheshire. *Peak* is in fact a misnomer, for it is plainly evident that peaks are in very short supply here: it derives from *Pecsaetan* ('hill-dweller'), tribes that occupied the area long before the Normans came.

The Peak divides into two distinctive areas, the Dark Peak and the White Peak. These refer to the principal rocks, millstone grit (gritstone) in the Dark Peak and limestone in the White Peak. The Dark Peak horseshoe encloses the limestone country, with the high moors of Kinder Scout and Bleaklow to the north and long arms reaching down either side. That in the east traces the Derwent Valley south in a series of abrupt edges: that to the west is disjointed, resurrecting itself above Buxton to run south, largely less dramatically, west of the Manifold Valley. The northern massif is typified by vast tracts of peat bog and heather, a world away from the White Peak's softer terrain.

The compact White Peak offers green dales overlooked by gleaming cliffs. Unlike the limestone country of the Yorkshire Dales, it has few potholes and pavements: its speciality is valleys, exemplified by the likes of Lathkill Dale, the river Wye and the incomparable Dovedale. Much of the White Peak is an upland plateau where old lead mining communities huddle. The area is dissected by drystone walls, and though large-scale quarrying is all too evident, farming remains the traditional source of employment, increasingly supplemented by tourism. While one railway survives to run through the heart of the Park, several others have been converted to leisure trails: they provide excellent cross-country routes linking numerous towns and villages.

Bakewell is the largest community in the National Park, but it is the small towns on the fringe, such as Buxton, Ashbourne, Matlock, Leek, Chapel en le Frith and Glossop, that act as major centres. Though this whole area might be encircled in a day's car tour, once you get out in the fresh air you will quickly appreciate the rich diversity of country that offers many happy years of real exploring - on foot.

SOUTHERN PEAK

The Southern Peak stretches from the river Dove to the Derwent, from the upland village of Longnor high on the fringes of limestone country to the deep wooded gorge of the Derwent at Matlock. The area is defined by Lathkill Dale to the north, the Derwent Valley to the east, Carsington Reservoir and the foot of Dovedale to the south, and the Dove itself to the west. Conveniently placed at each corner of the district are towns of varying size, namely Bakewell, Buxton, Ashbourne and Matlock. Of these, only the latter scrapes into these pages.

Within these bounds is an array of captivatingly diverse scenery, for while limestone predominates, pockets of millstone grit add immense variety, notably at Stanton Moor, Harthill Moor and the Black Rocks. History abounds: Arbor Low, just off two walks, is the most important archaeological site in the Peak; the Nine Ladies stone circle is a superb Bronze Age relic; and Pilsbury Castle is the finest local example of a motte and bailey castle site. Roystone Grange offers monastic interest, while Cromford is pre-eminent amongst Industrial Revolution sites. Another distinctive feature of the area are two old railways converted to leisure use: the High Peak Trail and the Tissington Trail cross the southern Peak offering easy or extended strolls amid grand scenery.

Countless attractive villages await exploration, Parwich, Alstonefield, Stanton in Peak and Ilam being four of the best. Monyash sits high on the limestone plateau, while delightful Tissington is one of England's finest. Lesser known places such as Brassington, Carsington and Bonsall lose nothing from being outside the National Park, and their lead mining history adds extra interest and character. Larger villages such as Youlgreave, Hartington, Longnor and Winster were once of far greater importance, and still have the evidence for those who seek it out. Almost without fail, these lovely locations feature welcoming examples of that great institution the village pub.

Lesser known valleys include Gratton Dale, Bradford Dale, Biggin Dale and Wensley Dale, but there is no denying the big two: Dovedale is the jewel in the Peak's crown and a magnet for visitors, rightly so for it truly is special. Dovedale proper however is but a short length, for upstream the Dove flows through Mill Dale, Wolfscote Dale and Beresford Dale, with many further unsung miles above Hartington. Running it a close second is beautiful Lathkill Dale, a much shorter valley that claims to have the purest waters in the land.

Access

Unlike the northern moors and eastern edges, which cover vast tracts of rolling moorland and are subject to numerous access agreements, the central and southern parts of the Peak have no such wide open spaces, but the area is extremely well covered by the extensive rights of way network. The small areas of truly open country that do exist already have good paths, so that the only times we resort to non rights of way are on odd occasions where concession paths have been negotiated or offered to open up popular areas. Examples in this book are Chrome Hill and the central section of Lathkill Dale. Additionally, the length of the Tissington and High Peak Trails are used in similar fashion.

Nine Ladies Stone Circle,
Stanton Moor

Please take extra care to respect the life and work of the Peak. Its very accessibility puts it in the firing line when we all want to escape into the country at the same time. If we take nothing more than photographs and leave only the slightest of footprints, then this wonderful landscape will be in good shape for the next generation. In particular, ensure that dogs are kept on leads and that you close any gates you have opened.

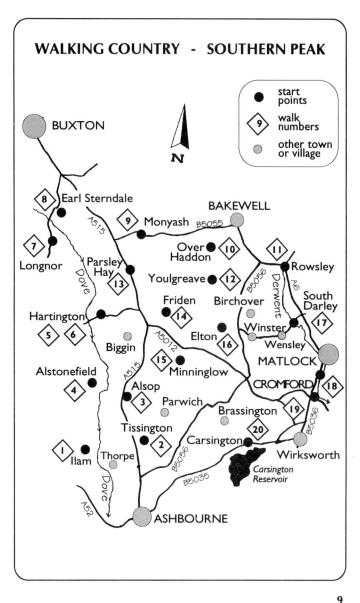

WALKING COUNTRY - SOUTHERN PEAK

start points

walk numbers 9

other town or village

N

BUXTON

8 Earl Sterndale

A515

9 Monyash B5055 BAKEWELL

7 Over Haddon 10 11

Longnor Parsley Hay Rowsley

Dove 13 Youlgreave 12 B5056 Derwent A6 South Darley

Friden Birchover 17

Hartington 14 Winster

5 6 Elton Wensley

Biggin A5012 16 MATLOCK

Alstonefield A515 15 Minninglow CROMFORD

4 Alsop 18

3 Parwich Brassington 19

Tissington Carsington 20

1 2 B5056 Wirksworth B5036

Ilam Thorpe Carsington Reservoir

Dove B5035

A52

ASHBOURNE

9

Getting around

This very compact region can be reached with ease from most places in the Peak District and surrounding towns. The four boundary towns mentioned overleaf would all make good bases, and all have good public transport links. Buxton and Matlock have the additional benefit of being railway termini. However, Bakewell to the north and Ashbourne to the south are perhaps more ideally placed for their respective areas.

Numerous seasonal bus services also operate on less regular routes. With a little planning, various permutations can be created by linking different sections of the walks, to create longer routes or to take advantage of public transport. Starting points with public transport, however limited, are indicated, along with other useful information, at the start of each walk.

Using the guide

Each walk is self-contained, with essential information being followed by a simple map and concise description of the route. Dovetailed between this are useful notes of features along the way, and interspersed are illustrations which both capture the flavour of the walks and record the many items of interest. In order to make the instructions easier to follow, essential route description has been highlighted in bold type, while items in lighter type refer to historical asides and things worth looking out for: in this format you can find your way more easily while still locating features of interest at the relevant point in the text.

The simple sketch maps identify the location of the routes rather than the fine detail, and whilst the route description should be sufficient to guide you around, an Ordnance Survey map is recommended: the route can easily be plotted on the relevant OS map. To gain the most from a walk, the detail of the 1:25,000 maps is unsurpassed. They also serve to vary walks as desired, giving an improved picture of one's surroundings and the availability of linking paths. Just one map gives complete coverage of the walks:-

• *Outdoor Leisure Sheet 24 - Peak District, White Peak*

Also extremely useful for general planning purposes are the Landranger maps at 1:50,000, and again, one sheet covers the entire area:

119, Buxton, Matlock & Dove Dale

One further planning aid is the OS Touring Map which covers the whole National Park at the scale of 1:63,360 (1 inch to the mile).

SOME USEFUL ADDRESSES

Ramblers' Association   1/5 Wandsworth Road, London SW8 2XX
Tel. 0171-582 6878

Peak National Park Office
Aldern House, Baslow Road, Bakewell DE45 1AE
Tel. 01629-816200

Bakewell Visitor Centre   Tel. 01629-813227

Hartington Old Signal Box Visitor Centre
(open weekends and BH Mondays, Easter-September)

Tourist Information
The Pavilion **Matlock Bath** Derbyshire DE4 3NR
Tel. 01629-55082
The Crescent **Buxton** Derbyshire SK17 6BQ
Tel. 01298-25106
Market Place **Leek** Staffordshire ST13 5HH
Tel. 01538-381000
Market Place **Ashbourne** Derbyshire DE6 1EU
Tel. 01335-343666

Peak & Northern Footpaths Society
Mr E Sutton, 1 Crossfield Grove, Marple Bridge, Cheshire SK6 5EQ
Tel. 0161-427 3582

Friends of National Parks
Council for National Parks, 246 Lavender Hill, London SW11 1LJ
Tel. 0171-924 4077

Derbyshire Wildlife Trust   Elvaston Castle, Derby DE7 3ET
Tel. 01332-756610

Staffordshire Wildlife Trust
Coutts House, Sandon, Stafford ST18 0DN   Tel. 01889-508534

The National Trust   South Peak Estate Office
Home Farm, Ilam, nr. Ashbourne, Derbyshire DE6 2AZ
Tel. 01335-350503

DOVEDALE

START *Ilam*   *Grid ref. SK 146509*

DISTANCE *4½ miles*

ORDNANCE SURVEY MAPS
1:50,000
Landranger 119 - Buxton, Matlock & Dove Dale
1:25,000
Outdoor Leisure 24 - Peak District, White Peak

ACCESS *Start from the cross in the centre of Ilam. There is a large National Trust car park at Ilam Hall country park. Served by market day buses from Ashbourne and Leek, and on Saturdays and Summer Sundays/BH Mondays by Ashbourne-Hanley express buses.*

If any walk deserves a quiet midweek, it is this one. You'll never get the place to yourself short of a pre-dawn start, but you'll certainly have room to move. Whenever you come though, it will be memorable.

S Ilam (pronounce it 'eye-lam') is an estate village of the Watts-Russell family. The hall was rebuilt in the 1820s as a brash Gothic mansion, but was demolished in 1934 and what survives now operates as a youth hostel. The Holy Cross church was restored in 1854 but retains some medieval elements. Inside a chapel is the tomb of St. Bertram, once a place of pilgrimage, while two Saxon crosses stand in the churchyard. The hall grounds are open to visitors as a country park, the National Trust have an information centre and shop in the hall's old cellar and a tearoom in the stable block.

From the car park return to the village centre, preferably by way of the church. The village centre is watched over by the elaborate Watts-Russell Memorial of 1840, also known as Ilam Cross. The hugely attractive school of 1854 is in the best tradition of the estate, along

12

with cottages and gardens that would grace many a chocolate box. The village bridge is the last on the Manifold: this often dry river springs back into life at the Boil Hole in the grounds of the hall - well worth a visit - and a mile further downstream it somewhat unjustly loses its name to the smaller Dove.

Leave the cross by the Dovedale road, briefly in the Manifold's company. After the last buildings go left through a gate onto the base of Bunster Hill. Slant up to a broad path and turn right along it. This continues beyond a stile and on through a couple of fields. Ahead is flat-topped Thorpe Cloud, appearing as if its cone has been sliced off by a giant knife. Like the peaks of WALK 8 near the head of the Dove, Thorpe Cloud and Bunster Hill are limestone reef knolls, formed in tropical seas more than 300 million years ago, and subsequently revealed when softer overlying rocks were gradually worn away.

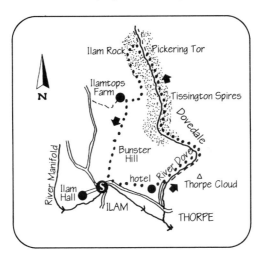

Pass along the back of the *Izaak Walton Hotel*. This rambling establishment recalls the 'father of fishing', author of the classic *The Compleat Angler* first published in 1653. Walton was a devotee of Dovedale and a regular visitor to the area, enjoying fishing excursions with his friend Charles Cotton. A stile gives access should you wish to visit the public bar. **The path runs to a stile and down to the large main car park.** Here are toilets and a refreshment van.

Go left past the limit of traffic and on to a footbridge on the Dove. A choice here, either the road on the left or the path on the base of Thorpe Cloud will lead upstream to the celebrated Stepping Stones. Here those on the road side have the occasional benefit of an ice cream van, but must then cross the stones to resume upstream. No description of the route is required for the next two miles, and the sheer beauty of the scenery almost defies description. This anti-clockwise route has two major advantages: a) the dramatic entry into the valley, and b) slowly but surely most of the crowds are shaken off as they are forced to about turn to their cars!

The finest features en route are indicated on the OS map. Another regular feature is the string of weirs which creates pools for the fish to gather when the water levels are low. When the path rises to a scrappy knoll at **Lover's Leap** the **Twelve Apostles** are identifiable across the river as a gathering of assembled tors sprouting from the greenery. After this is the stepped monolith of **Jacob's Ladder**, then the rocky pinnacles of **Tissington Spires** form the skyline on our right. A little further, a massive natural arch frames the dark hole of **Reynard's Cave** behind it: all the while, the delectable Dove gurgles away. The tight ravine of the Straits follows, with the path forced onto boardwalks. By a cleft on the right, easily missed is a tiny plaque to a man whose vision secured much of this property for the National Trust.

Possibly the finest moment, and appropriately just before we take our leave, is arrival at a pair of improbable tors on each side of a footbridge on the river. The pinnacled blade of rock on the right is **Pickering Tor**, tilting back skywards, secreting a cave at its base, while on the other bank the remarkable **Ilam Rock** thrusts into the skies. Each of these towers virtually 100ft into the air: quite incredible!

The bridge beneath Ilam Rock is the first since the Stepping Stones. Cross and turn upstream for two minutes to find a departing path a little further than its original route. Signed to Ilam, it begins a cleverly worked spiral up through the trees, making relatively light work of the contours.

At the top the path runs left above Dovedale Wood. This fine walk runs above a superb example of surviving ash and wych elm, and offers glimpses through to limestone scenery below and opposite. **Eventually the path reaches the end, and (not as per map) passes through successive ladder-stiles and along a farm track to the**

buildings ahead. Views from here lead the eye to Thorpe Cloud and out of Dovedale to the lowlands behind. **Don't enter the farmyard, but go left around the fence above the steep bank. Just past Air Cottage (which has associations with the writer D. H. Lawrence), turn right over a fence-stile and up the paddock to a small gate. Now turn left on the drive rising away towards Ilamtops Farm.**

At the gateway don't advance to the house, but take the track sharp left. This rises, briefly enclosed to emerge alongside a barn. Yet again not as per map, advance along the wall-side to a stile at the end. This accesses the back of Bunster Hill. The National Trust footpath turns right down the wall-side, descending the western flank of the hill. Part way down we pass St. Bertram's Well, where a tiny spring gurgles into a stone surround. Ahead are good views over the Ilam scene. **The slopes broaden out near the bottom, and passing above the pond a broader track runs on to meet the outward route at the base of the hill. Conclude the walk as it began.**

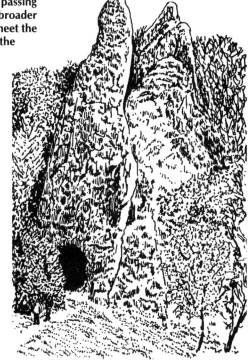

Pickering Tor,
Dovedale

THORPE CLOUD

START *Tissington*   *Grid ref. SK 178520*

DISTANCE *6½ miles*

ORDNANCE SURVEY MAPS
1:50,000
Landranger 119 - Buxton, Matlock & Dove Dale
1:25,000
Outdoor Leisure 24 - Peak District, White Peak

ACCESS *Start from the National Park's Tissington Trail car park in the village, off the A515. Served by market day buses from Ashbourne, otherwise the main road at Tissington Gates very infrequently, including Summer Sunday/BH Monday Buxton-Ashbourne buses. Alternative starts are the main Dovedale car park west of Thorpe, and the Thorpe station car park on the Tissington Trail east of the village.*

Lots of ups and downs in charming country near the foot of Dovedale, with an optional ascent of its symbolic guardian offering outstanding views. The last section links two attractive villages by way of the Tissington Trail.

❺ From the car park entrance turn left into the village. Tissington is a delightfully laid out estate village, acclaimed as one of England's finest. It is normally approached from Tissington Gates on the main road, along a half-mile parkland lime avenue. Tissington Hall is a large mansion dating back to Jacobean times, and home of the Fitzherberts for more than 400 years. Across the broad street, St. Mary's church sits anciently on a knoll, its sturdy, mainly Norman tower complemented by an interior featuring numerous impressive memorials to the Fitzherbert family. The village has a great sense of space with open grassy areas abounding: a duckpond is centrally placed outside the little Post office/shop.

Tissington is best known as the home of well dressing, an ancient pagan ritual revived here in the 18th century or possibly earlier, with a Christian theme. A more modern revival has seen the tradition expand so that today it is replicated in countless villages across the White Peak. This endearing feature may be an undoubted tourist attraction, but it nevertheless also serves to draw local communities together. The custom dates back to the days when grateful thanks were offered for a pure water supply, something not to be taken for granted in a limestone district. As such, communities went to great lengths to preserve and respect their indispensable wells, and this took the form of 'dressing' it in a wide variety of floral styles.

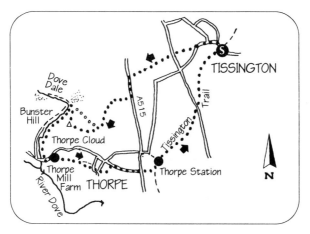

Well dressing is a time consuming craft: subjects vary from year to year and village to village, but the underlying theme is giving praise for God's gifts. Pressed into a clay base are petals, berries, seeds, mosses - almost anything nature can supply, depending on the season. Events take place over several months between May and September. Tissington's five wells are traditionally the first blessed, on Ascension Day, and displays remain in place for a week or so - being living things their lifespan is naturally limited!

The five wells are Coffin Well, Hands Well, Hall Well, Town Well and Yew Tree Well. The first is passed on the right, at the first green, while the latter is last feature on the left before leaving the village. The other three line the main street on and past the hall.

Keep left past the triangle and on out of the village. Crossing a cattle-grid accessing the avenue through Tissington Park, leave at once and follow the rising wall on the right. After a second stile bear left over the brow to a stile onto the main road. The *Bluebell Inn* stands just past Tissington Gates, to the south. Advance straight across and down the field to a stile in the bottom. Selective winter snow throws the medieval ridge and furrow ploughing of fields hereabouts into stark relief. Bear left to the top of the wall then across to a gate just behind. Rise to a stile and continue to climb steeply by the wallside. On the brow the wall turns off: keep straight on to a stile onto a narrow road. Go left, enjoying good views all around from this modest ridge.

Thorpe Cloud from the stepping stones, Dovedale

A gate admits the road onto the open terrain of the National Trust's Thorpe Pastures. At once strike up to the right. The brow reveals the first real prospect of Thorpe Cloud just ahead, here resembling a table mountain. Signs warning not to enter when red flags are flying make a suitable disclaimer for the firing range down in the bottom. In this instance the prudent might wish to continue down the road to a footpath branching off beyond Pike House.

Descend past a dewpond into the dry valley below, and before the firing range contour right to gain the neck of land leading out to Hamston Hill. The constantly improving scene is dominated by Thorpe Cloud, with the slopes of Bunster Hill, to its right, hovering above Dovedale. **After a possible detour onto Hamston Hill, drop down to the wall corner at the back of Thorpe Cloud.** If not wishing to scale this mini-peak, turn down to the right on a broadening footpath through Lin Dale to enter Dovedale almost at the Stepping Stones.

To climb Thorpe Cloud, go left outside the wall from the corner, rising gently to a kissing-gate giving access to the hill. A path quickly forms to make a short ascent to the top, where a rocky bluff offers a mild scramble before promenading along the little crest to the dramatic perch above the valley, at a height of 941ft/287m. Almost vertically below is the entrance to Dovedale, where the celebrated Stepping Stones see the path off up the dale between deep-cut, wooded flanks. Opposite, Bunster Hill, our twin portal, is particularly impressive with its scarred limestone flanks. 'Cloud', incidentally, derives from the old English *clud*, meaning rock or hill.

The descent path drops down to the right (north), winding unfailingly down to meet the valley path at the foot of Lin Dale. Do not wander elsewhere, as the Dovedale flank is excessively steep and dangerous, and there is a need to preserve the hill from further erosion. On gaining the dale floor it is tempting to wander upstream, as far as you might wish, and WALK 1 does exactly this. Thorpe Cloud itself now towers above most impressively, to say the least.

Our return route turns left, down the path along the very base of Thorpe Cloud. Alternatively, cross the Stepping Stones and follow the narrow road down the other bank as far as a footbridge: the main Dovedale car park, with toilets and usually refreshments, is just a minute or two further along the lane.

Reaching a footbridge, leave the drama by a stile in front and continue downstream, now in sedate surroundings. Several stiles lead to a dry millcut, deflecting us from the river to a stile onto a road alongside the millcut bridge. Go left to Thorpe Mill Farm, and at a cattle-grid immediately past it the road becomes unenclosed. Climb the steep field to a waiting gap-stile on the skyline.

Advance across the fields above to the very far end, where a gap-stile by a gate admits onto the head of a lane alongside a house. Take a rickety gap just opposite, in front of the house, and bear right across the field: ahead are the scattered houses of Thorpe. A series of stiles lead along to a short-lived snicket between houses out onto a narrow road. The large Manor House stands to the right. **Bear right on the road to reach the church.** St. Leonard's little church is dominated by its solid Norman tower, the rest having been rebuilt in 1881. A 1767 sundial can be found in the churchyard.

An enclosed way runs to the left of the church, dropping below the churchyard to a path junction. Turn left, down a wooded dell to run on, across a dribbling stream to join a back road. Turn right up this narrow way, quickly easing out at farm buildings. Be sure to look back to see Thorpe Cloud resembling a true, conical peak. **A T-junction is reached just ahead.** A pub, the *Dog & Partridge* stands a couple of minutes along to the left. **The route crosses straight over and bears right to the next stile. Descend the field to a kissing-gate onto the Tissington Trail.**

Turn left along the old railway to lead unfailingly back to the start, a stroll of a little under two miles. En route we pass the car park and station house at the former Thorpe station; through Fenny Bentley Cutting (a nature reserve of Derbyshire Wildlife Trust); and over the main road and through a longer cutting, at the end of which Tissington village appears ahead. For more on the former railway and trail to which Tissington gave its name, please see WALK 13.

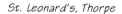

St. Leonard's, Thorpe

MILL DALE

START *Alsop en le Dale*　　　　*Grid ref. SK 155549*

DISTANCE *5½ miles*

ORDNANCE SURVEY MAPS
1:50,000
Landranger 119 - Buxton, Matlock & Dove Dale
1:25,000
Outdoor Leisure 24 - Peak District, White Peak

ACCESS *Start from the National Park's Alsop en le Dale (Tissington Trail) Station car park on the A515 north of Tissington. Infrequent buses include Ashbourne-Buxton services (Sunday & BH Monday).*

A plunge from the Tissington Trail into the splendour of the Dove.

S Alsop station on the London & North Western Railway's Buxton to Ashbourne line served the equally small village of Alsop en le Dale, nestling in a hollow far below: our walk seems far removed from the village, of which we don't even catch a glimpse. Now converted to the Tissington Trail, for more on the line please refer to WALK 13.

Return to the main road, cross at the junction and take a stile just to the left. Bear left down the field to a stile at the end. Cross over the road (Green Lane) and up the farm road opposite, rising past New Hanson Grange to a brow. During this stage there are revealing views north into the deep confines of the Dove, with steep wooded flanks secreting mysterious folds in the hills. Up to our left is the tree-topped knoll of Moat Low, site of a Bronze Age barrow (burial chamber).

Descend towards the farm at Hanson Grange, but before it bear left across the field to a stile. Slant across to another wall, and if the stile is missing it is easier to drop down to a gate in front of the farmhouse.

Head away left on a track, almost at once turning down off it to enter the head of wooded Nabs Dale. A good path winds down this steep, crag-flanked side valley to join the main valley of the Dove. Just to the left are the yawning caverns of Dove Holes, mighty twin black holes with a central pillar (illustrated on page 26).

Our way goes right, upstream on the main valley path through glorious surroundings. Prominent on the opposite bank is the tall climbers' cliff of Raven's Tor, while a limestone pinnacle also towers above us. The path runs on to arrive at Viator's Bridge, Milldale. For more on Milldale, please see page 26. There are two options here. The direct route crosses the bridge into the hamlet and follows the road updale to Lode Mill.

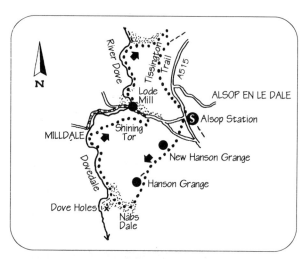

The more demanding walk to Lode Mill makes a steep start but offers revealing views from Pinch Bank. Without crossing the bridge take a path climbing right, numerous zigzags outwitting the gradient. Level with the wood top, leave the rising path and bear left to the start of the wall, overlooking the valley. Rise more gently with this to the brow, and take a stile. A super path runs on above the steep bank. In this fine prospect of the valley below, Lode Mill quickly appears. Remain on this path with a wall to the right, curving round above Lode Mill and briefly heading away from our objective.

Above Shining Tor we look directly up the valley past Lode Mill, a magnificent scene of overlapping spurs. Even on a busy day there is no sign of the Dovedale crowds, indeed this could be almost anywhere. **When the path turns in around the head of a dry hollow, a path crossroads is met at a couple of stiles. Turn down to the left with the wall for a short, easy descent to the road.** The guidepost pointing down the road advises '*Lode Mill avoiding road*'!

Go left for a couple of minutes down to Lode Mill. This is a grand spot, with the old mill and a couple of cottages sharing a riverside setting by the bridge. **Take the path upstream, which now clings to the riverbank for a long mile.** Small stone weirs punctuate the river at regular intervals, creating pools for the fish at times of low water. **After an open spell on the right a branch path turns away as the woods restart by a stone waterworks building.**

Lode Mill,
Mill Dale

Here forsake the Dove and turn up the branch path, climbing the hollow outside the trees. Above, the modest limestone outcrops of Bradbury's Bank draw us into the narrow defile. The going eases, and just beyond the end of the wood we finally reach the end of the pasture. Here double sharply back to the right on a well made old path, slanting up and slowly fading before reaching a small gateway and stile in the top corner.

Advance to the railway arch ahead. During this last spell there are some grand views down over our side valley into the main dale. **A farm track is met in front of the arch: don't go under but cross to the path slanting up the railway embankment. Turn right along the Tissington Trail for less than a mile's steady walk, passing under the main road just before the end.**

4

RIVER DOVE

START *Alstonefield*   *Grid ref. SK 130555*

DISTANCE *6¼ miles*

ORDNANCE SURVEY MAPS
1:50,000
Landranger 119 - Buxton, Matlock & Dove Dale
1:25,000
Outdoor Leisure 24 - Peak District, White Peak

ACCESS *Start from the village centre. There is a small car park by the toilets with more space on the road alongside. Served by Ashbourne-Buxton buses on Sundays/BH Mondays, and on market days from Ashbourne and Leek.*

An idyllic village sets the scene for the splendour of the Dove in and around Milldale. A real gem of a walk.

S Alstonefield is a beautiful village further enriched by a dazzling springtime daffodil display. Everywhere are green spaces, with the focal point being the green outside the village pub, the *George*. Nearby are tearooms and a Post Office/store. St. Peter's church stands in an 'Olde Englande' village setting, with the vicarage in close proximity. Prize feature inside the church is the woodwork, from the dark carved oak box pews of 1639 to the imposing pulpit. The hall bears a 1587 datestone and was originally the rectory.

From the car park go right to the road junction, then up onto the green in front of the pub. Go straight past the greens (south) on the church lane. Just before the vicarage a narrow snicket takes a path off to the right between walls. This quickly emerges into a field. Head directly away with a fence, over a stile and up the field to a corner-stile in the wall. Ignoring the rough walled lane we join, enter the

field on the left and descend the wall-side to the corner. **Ahead are the slopes enclosing the Dove. Slant down to the right to a stile above a steep bank, then a clear path descends onto the narrow road through Hope Dale.**

Cross straight over and up the walled track of Brunister Lane opposite. This climbs (again lined by daffodils in season) to a brow. Look back to see Alstonefield church across the deep trough. **Continue on to emerge at a road junction at Stanshope.** The striking red brick frontage of 17th century Stanshope Hall looks odd in this limestone setting, but nevertheless very attractive.

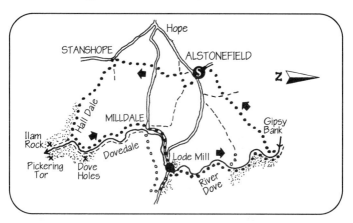

Without setting foot on the road turn sharp left along a rough lane, leaving at the first opportunity at a stile on the right. The head of Hall Dale is straight ahead, and a path slants through the fields to reach it. The way then makes a straightforward descent of this dry valley to join the Dove. The stroll down Hall Dale is increasingly colourful as we are swallowed up by steeper flanks and the enticing prospect of the main valley's many charms. The Dove is reached in glorious surroundings of woodland and limestone.

While the suggested route goes left, those who have not seen Ilam Rock and Pickering Tor may wish to go right for a few minutes down to a footbridge beneath the said pillars (see WALK 1): from here one could simply follow the main path up the east bank to Milldale. **Those still with me can turn upstream at once, a thin path contrasting**

**markedly with the hard surfaced and heavily populated one oppo-
site.** Almost at once we squeeze beneath a limestone wall, and if the
river is high we might all have to go downstream to the footbridge!
Otherwise forge on up-dale through outstanding scenery, richly
wooded and decorated by limestone crags and outcrops. **The yawning caverns of Dove Holes are passed across the river.** These mighty
black holes with a central pillar are well displayed from our bank.

Dove Holes

**The way meanders the water's edge for some time, passing beneath
the 130ft climbers' cliff of Raven's Tor and by a series of springs. The
dale opens out a little, loses its cragginess, and the path does the
unthinkable and leaves it. Rising through several stiles to below a
tiny barn, this offers new perspectives on the valley. Here slant up
the field to a stile into woods, quickly leaving them again and
working round above more trees on Achas Bank to approach the
hamlet of Milldale.**

Arrival here is reminiscent of reaching a hidden cove on a coastal
path, sudden and dramatic above the cramped settlement. **A little
path winds down to enter the hamlet.** Interest centres around Viator's
Bridge, one of the finest examples of a packhorse bridge in the Peak.
Alongside is the restored sheepwash, last used in 1965 for washing
fleeces at shearing time. A National Trust information barn with
panels imparts much of local interest; there are also toilets and just
along the side road a shop sells refreshments. An optional high level
route to Lode Mill is described in WALK 3.

This point marks the northern limit of Dovedale proper, and here Mill Dale takes over. **Resume upstream, briefly on a 'disabled' access path before leaving the houses behind to spend ten minutes on the road. A pathway is incorporated part-way along.** We still have the river's company all the way, with small stone weirs at regular intervals for fish to gather when the water is in short supply. **Beyond a road junction Lode Mill is quickly reached.** This is a grand spot, with the old mill (illustrated on page 23) and a couple of cottages sharing a riverside setting by the bridge.

Cross the bridge and take the path upstream, which now clings to the riverbank for a long mile. Weirs remain in constant attendance, and it's still fine stuff. **After an open spell on the right a branch path turns away as woods restart behind a stone waterworks building: Coldeaton footbridge crosses the river on the left. Keep on until arrival at two sets of stepping stones, further identified by a small stone shelter on the right, beneath the craggy bluff of Iron Tors.** Here was the site of a ram pump house, built to pump water to farmland above, and worked by water action.

Firstly, it is worth advancing to the stile out of the trees just ahead to enjoy a superb setting on the riverbank where Wolfscote Dale and Biggin Dale split, one carrying the Dove, the other contrastingly dry (see WALK 5). Up to the right above the stile is a cave. **NB:** If the river level should make the stepping stones hazardous, return to Coldeaton footbridge. An alternative path crosses and climbs away towards Alstonefield.

Having crossed the stepping stones face up to a stiff path up Gipsy Bank. The views back are good so there's plenty of excuse to halt! **At the top it winds round to the left, giving stunning views down-dale as it runs along to a stile into the fields. Head away to a stile in front, then slant left through a couple of fields towards a barn ahead. Go right to the barn where a firm track is joined, this leading out to a junction.** The village has by now appeared just ahead.

Cross to a stile opposite, then down the field. Past a crumbling wall take a stile on the right, and cross to a gate near the far corner. Joining a track, the path meticulously takes a couple of stiles just ahead to cross a small paddock, then rejoining the track to go left onto the road. Go left to finish.

5

WOLFSCOTE DALE & BIGGIN DALE

START Hartington   Grid ref. SK 128604

DISTANCE 5¾ miles

ORDNANCE SURVEY MAPS
1:50,000
Landranger 119 - Buxton, Matlock & Dove Dale
1:25,000
Outdoor Leisure 24 - Peak District, White Peak

ACCESS Start from the village centre. There is a car park at the western end, and also some parking in the square. Served by bus from Buxton, and occasionally from Ashbourne, Leek and, seasonally, places further afield.

Very easy walking through two superb but contrasting limestone valleys, on the edge of Hartington yet well hidden. The first is a dry paradise, the other gives us the Dove.....

S Hartington is one of the best known villages of the White Peak. It stands at the head of the most dramatic miles of the river Dove, and the riverbank walk here from Thorpe Cloud is one of the classics of the land. Its spacious centre is spread around a square, and features of interest include millpond, cheese shop, cafes, 1902 Coronation water tap, restaurant and two pubs, the *Devonshire Arms* and the *Charles Cotton Hotel*.

The latter honours the great fishing companion of Izaak Walton, author of the time-honoured *The Compleat Angler* first published in 1653. Cotton (1630-1687) lived nearby (we shall pass nearer at the end of the walk) and Walton came to visit him for their celebrated

28

fishing expeditions. He considered the Dove the finest river in the land. In 1676 Cotton added his own chapter to the famous manual. To balance things up, Walton himself is remembered by a hotel at the foot of Dovedale. The fine old market hall sports a Latin datestone of 1836 and now incorporates a shop. A house alongside bears a 1777 datestone. The parish church of St. Giles stands just above, dating back to the 14th century and boasting an impressive tower. Hartington is also known for its Stilton cheese factory, a major local employer sending its produce far beyond the bounds of the Dove.

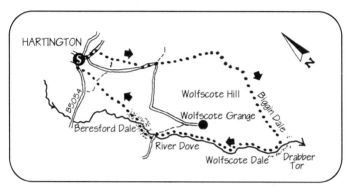

Leave the market square by heading east, and opposite the church lane turn right at the war memorial. The road is signposted to the youth hostel and passes a former chapel of 1809 as it climbs steeply to it. The hostel occupies Hartington Hall, which dates back to 1350 when it served the nuns of St. Clare. It was substantially rebuilt in 1611 by the Bateman family, and it is said Bonnie Prince Charlie stayed here on his abortive march south in 1745. The hall became one of the country's first hostels and a copper beech alongside the drive was planted by Richard Schirmann, founder of the youth hostelling movement. The hugely attractive building is well worth an overnight stay to discover some of its fine internal features.

Turn off along a rough lane to the right opposite the hall. This runs pleasantly on as a green way between limestone walls: when it turns sharp right, keep straight on the lesser way, still between old walls. Terminating in a field corner, slant down to the crumbling wall opposite, passing through and continuing on to a stile in the far corner. This admits to a narrow road.

Go left to a junction and keep straight on the rough lane ahead. Passing a barn it improves into a footway and begins a steady descent into one of the upper arms of Biggin Dale. Drop down to the dry valley floor and turn right on the green carpet. This quickly swings in left to a stile and circular concrete mere at the junction of arms. The main path goes right with the wall, now commencing a journey through the floor of Biggin Dale, a nature reserve.

The way is clear throughout as it leads unerringly to a junction with the river Dove at the foot of Wolfscote Dale. Features en route include a dark cave entrance on the left, an adit from lead mining days. This horizontal hole can be penetrated for some distance, though absence of a torch will ensure you can't go too far. Every step towards the Dove is sheer delight, amidst scrubby wooded flanks and limestone outcrops and scree.

Arrival at the Dove is an out-standing moment that will cause you to stop in your tracks. All around are limestone delights,

Drabber Tor, Wolfscote Dale

though the lush bank of the river is perhaps the finest attraction after our dry valley. Across the river are limestone cliffs featuring the fine pinnacles of Drabber Tor. It is worth passing through the stile to savour the glorious section immediately downstream. Up above on the left note the large dark cave entrance.

Hartington Hall

Back at the junction, turn right up the riverside, travelling an enchanting course on a firm path up the entire length of Wolfscote Dale. More fine tors shoot up from the slopes opposite. **After a craggy finale, a pronounced end is reached at a bridge where an old lane crosses the river. Don't cross the bridge, but advance to a stile and cross a meadow upstream to another footbridge. Here Beresford Dale begins: cross the bridge to the road end then turn sharp right to follow the woodland path up-dale.**

Beresford Dale is a mere half-mile in length, a wooded, almost hidden mini-dale. **A footbridge crosses midway, just after an intriguing 18ft pinnacle at Pike Pool.** High above the rocky walls opposite are glimpses of a dramatically sited prospect tower, better seen on looking back in a few minutes' time. It stands within the grounds of what was Beresford Hall, and was restored in 1906 using stone from the old hall. The hall itself was once the home of Charles Cotton.

The path rises away from the river and out of the wood. Its course remains clear for this final stage through the fields, rising to cross a rough little lane and on to emerge back into the village alongside the toilets and a pottery.

PILSBURY CASTLE

6

START Hartington   Grid ref. SK 128604

DISTANCE 6 miles

ORDNANCE SURVEY MAPS
1:50,000
Landranger 119 - Buxton, Matlock & Dove Dale
1:25,000
Outdoor Leisure 24 - Peak District, White Peak

ACCESS Start from the village centre. There is a car park at the western end, and also some parking in the square. Served by bus from Buxton, and occasionally from Ashbourne, Leek and, seasonally, places further afield.

A gentle walk up-dale from Hartington, into quieter, more open landscapes than WALK 5, which goes south with the Dove. The goal is an atmospheric historic site. For more on Hartington please refer to the above mentioned walk.

S **Leave the square by heading up the side road towards the church. At the top turn left on a road climbing steeply out of the village. Remain on this for a short mile, ever rising past the last isolated houses. After a house on the right, a path branches left at the head of an old lane. Ignore this and continue up to a new house on the left. On the bend above, a stile sets us off above a modern barn. Cross to the next stile, slant down to the next, then bear left onto a barns drive. Pass through the gate below with it, and down just as far as a hairpin bend with Bank Top Farm below.**

Leave the track on the bend and go straight on through a gate, and walk on increasingly pleasantly along the top of the bank. When the wall parts company, forge straight on across this attractive, vast

open pasture with occasional limestone and scrub. One or two waymarkers may be in evidence. **Passing a length of crumbling wall another section leads to a crumbling facing wall, and on through a smaller field (a path crossroads on the map) to another stile ahead.**

By this stage shapely eminences up towards the dalehead have appeared, including the classic pairing of Chrome and Parkhouse Hills. Note also the contrast of rock from our limestone to the gritstone country across the dale: a very different landscape. **Forge on again on a faint trod over the brow, and from the next stile slant up a couple of fields to ruinous barns in the trees above.**

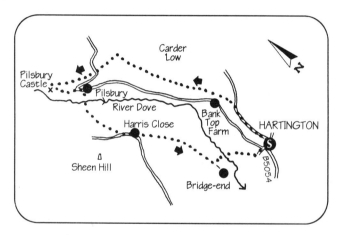

The track along the front goes to a gate just to the left. Here leave the track and slant up to a wall corner, then up again to another. Now advance on with a crumbling wall to locate a stile in the descending wall ahead. Through it a path drops steeply down a wallside to a stile and path crossroads in a hollow. Turn left here, through the minor hollow and out onto a narrow road. Pilsbury is just down to the left, but our way crosses to a stile opposite and bears left to another two in succession.

Over the dale note the fine twin gabled house at Broadmeadow Hall. **Advance along the brow with the wall until it parts company. At this point slant left to join a green way down to another green wallside track just in front of the castle site.** This finest view reveals more of the mini peaks updale, beyond the castle site itself set amongst Pilsbury Castle Hills. The well defined, grassy fortifications of the Norman (and possibly older) motte and bailey castle are best accentuated in long evening shadows. This is the finest such relic in the Peak, even incorporating a natural tor.

Though a stile gives access via the continuing path, our route doubles back left on the inviting wallside way, which gradually becomes firmer as it runs on to a hairpin bend on the road through Pilsbury. Turn down it past the farm. An imposing three-storey house is focal point of this farming hamlet astride an old salters' way crossing the Peak. Our route used a brief section of this old packhorse route above the hamlet, and also in this next stage down to the river. **Leave the road by a broad green way down to the right. This descends to a ford and footbridge on the river Dove.**

The track resumes up the other side, but at the first chance take a stile on the left into a large pasture. Slant steeply up to the far side, odd trods pointing the way to a gap-stile in the rising wall. Enjoy good views back up-dale, with the castle itself well seen. **Go left with a crumbling wall to a stile in it, then rise again through two further stiles towards a house above. Pass left to a corner stile out onto a road.** The rocky knoll of Sheen Hill is very prominent up to the right.

Go left for a few minutes to Harris Close Farm at the corner. Turn into the yard but then sharply right of all buildings, squeezing past to emerge into a field. Now simply follow the right-hand wall through several fields until the wall ends. Here keep straight on to drop down to the next stile and resume with the wall as before. Hartington is outspread ahead. We now savour an improved situation with a modest but steep grassy edge beneath us. **The path runs on to a plantation, running through the top to a stile at the end. Here slant left on the path down a gorse bank to join a firm track. Go right just as far as a path junction before the farm at Bridge-end, and take a stile on the left.**

Descend the field centre to a footbridge back over the Dove, then slant right to a stile with a wall-stile behind. The way is now obvious as it cuts through the fields to the left of the cheese factory. The path runs past the buildings and onto its access road. Go left to re-enter the village.

7

TWO RIVERS

START *Longnor*   *Grid ref. SK 088649*

DISTANCE *4¾ miles*

ORDNANCE SURVEY MAPS
1:50,000
Landranger 119 - Buxton, Matlock & Dove Dale
1:25,000
Outdoor Leisure 24 - Peak District, White Peak

ACCESS *Start from the village centre. Various sensible car parking options. Served by Buxton-Hartington buses, and less frequently from Leek.*

A simple stroll around the upper reaches of the Dove and Manifold, two famous rivers that run parallel through many more famous miles downstream, but earn little attention in these unfrequented reaches.

🅢 . Sat high on a ridge twixt Dove and Manifold, Longnor was once a market town of some stature. Its centrally placed market hall of 1873 confirms it was such until relatively recently: a preserved 1903 table of market traders' tolls is still in place beneath the gable. The building now houses an enterprising craft centre with refreshments. There are also tearooms in the chippy next door. Longnor's status is also reflected in the fact that four pubs survive, though how it sustains this number is a mystery. St. Bartholomew's church dates from 1780, while there is also a Wesleyan Chapel of 1855. A former Methodist Chapel now serves as a doll's hospital!

From the market hall head east along the road past the *Cheshire Cheese* pub. Almost at the end of the village a little road slips down to the right into the yard of Fold Ends Farm. Turn left between the buildings and out into a field. The path drops to the bottom corner

where it splits. **One branch can be seen running across the fields ahead, indicated by a series of gap-stiles. Our preferred way drops down to a prominent gap-stile in the wall below. From it turn downstream with the Manifold, which is largely hidden from our sights.**

The path runs on through several fields, erring a little away from the river before meeting a farm drive. Turn left to follow it up to the house at Over Boothlow. Entering the yard, go up to the left to rise between outbuildings to another path junction. This time rise straight up to a gate, from were a sunken way slants left up the field. Enjoy sweeping views over the Manifold Valley to Longnor, across to Revidge, down to Ecton and Wetton Hills, and across to Axe Edge.

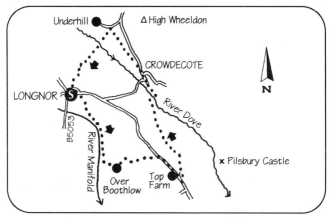

At the top take the right-hand gate, and the old track slants up again. Meeting a wall it runs up its side to the top, where it heads away as a walled lane to join the Longnor-Sheen road. Two minutes along to the left is Knowsley Cross, an ancient shaft and base restored in 1899. **Our way turns right along the road for ten minutes, enjoying wide views over two valleys as we prepare to transfer to the Dove scene.**

Beyond Top Farm a drive goes off to the left. 120 yards further, before a junction, take a stile on the left and double sharply back to a gap-stile. Cross to another which gives access to the aforementioned drive. Down to the right the shapely mounds of Pilsbury Castle can be discerned in the dale bottom: these are the remains of a Norman motte and bailey fort visited in WALK 6. Ahead, the cone of High Wheeldon shelters our objective of Crowdecote.

Follow the drive down to the first house at Under Whitle. The path is signed left, above the house to a stile then along the base of a scrubby bank. At the end join another drive on a hairpin (not on the map) at a myriad of notices. Go right, quickly leaving as directed by the path contouring left. Beyond a small pond keep on to a gap in the scrub, where slant down to a restored barn. Pass above it to a stile onto its access track. Go left, but as it starts to climb to Upper Whitle (the farm above) take a stile on the right and head off with the wall to a corner stile.

Slant down the big pasture to find a tiny bridge, then head away with a hedge. When it turns off keep straight on to finally join the Dove at a stile. Advance to the next stile, but just before it turn down to a footbridge on the river with a farm behind. Across the bridge, with its old ford, rise onto a back lane. Go left on here to enter tiny Crowdecote, with the *Pack Horse Inn* on the right.

Just yards past the pub, turn left along a side road. At the end of the houses turn down a drive which runs parallel with the road past farm buildings. At the end it runs on as an enclosed track to emerge into a field. Ahead rise the ruggedly majestic Chrome and Parkhouse Hills. Keep straight on the right side, with wall then fence to a corner stile. Continue along the wallside to a stile onto the corner of a back road. Without setting foot on it, turn left along the splendid wide green way of Green Lane.

Green Lane drops down to cross the Dove at Beggar's Bridge, a simple footbridge. The path rises up the bank opposite, passing a spring to join a track behind a barn. Up-dale, the peaks of Chrome and Parkhouse Hills look as good as ever. **Rise up and within 100 yards take an old stile on the right. A green path escapes the gorse bank to zigzag up to a stile at the brow. Cross the field to a stile and gate from where a leafy pathway drops down into the village.**

TABLE OF TOLLS PAYABLE AT
LONGNOR MARKETS and FAIRS
BY SELLERS

For every stall not exceeding six feet in length	
For every stall exceeding six feet in length, per foot additional	Four pence
For every pen of sheep, pigs or other live stock	One penny
For every standing for a Cart or carriage containing any article for sale	Four pence
For every standing without a carriage	Four pence
For every basket of eggs or other articles for sale	One penny
For all cheese, ducks or poultry not in baskets, per score	One penny
	Two pence

BY BUYERS

For every horse	
For every cow or bull two years old	Four pence
For every cow or bull under two years old	Two pence
For every sheep	One penny
For every pig	One halfpenny
	One penny

By Order of Sir Vauncy Harpur Crewe, BART.
LORD of the Manor of LONGNOR
August 1903   John Shaw, Agent

*Toll board,
Longnor
Market Hall*

8

CHROME HILL

START *Earl Sterndale*   *Grid ref. SK 090670*

DISTANCE *5¼ miles*

ORDNANCE SURVEY MAPS
1:50,000
Landranger 119 - Buxton, Matlock & Dove Dale
1:25,000
Outdoor Leisure 24 - Peak District, White Peak

ACCESS *Start from the village centre. Reasonable roadside parking. Served by Buxton-Hartington buses, and from further afield on Summer Sundays/BH Mondays.*

An absorbing stroll around the remarkable limestone peaks that bestow unique character on these upper reaches of the river Dove. The traverse of Chrome Hill is on a concession path.

S Earl Sterndale is perhaps best known for its odd pub name. The *Quiet Woman* is not a contradiction in terms, but stems from a previous landlord losing patience with his wife's tongue. His solution to the problem is depicted on the pub sign, along with the words *Soft Words Turneth Away Wrath* - too late for her, surely! Centrepiece is the village green overlooked by the church. This modest structure of local stone with a somewhat spartan interior dates only from 1952, its predecessor having been struck by enemy action in 1941 during an attack on a munitions dump above Buxton. Along the street is a shop with refreshments, and a Methodist chapel of 1850.

From the green cross to the pub and turn along to the right into a menagerie yard. At once a path fork is reached, to which we shall return at the end. Go right to a stile in the top corner and away through several small enclosures. Emerging into a field bear left,

over the brow to find a stile in the bottom corner. During this crossing we are greeted by the prospect of what are surely Alpine peaks: the improbable Parkhouse Hill soars skywards for all its 1230ft/ 375m or so can sustain, while behind it rises Chrome Hill, less stunning, for now... These limestone reef knolls were formed in tropical seas more than 300 million years ago, and subsequently revealed when softer overlying rocks were gradually worn away.

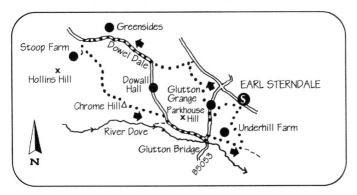

From the stile cross to one in the wall below, then a thin path descends the pasture to a stile at the bottom, and slant left to one onto the narrow back road in Glutton Dale. Turn right to Glutton Grange. This sturdy, three-storey farmhouse bears a circular 1675 datestone. **Turn into the yard, passing left of the house and keeping right of all buildings to the end. Take the right-hand gate into a field and head away with the wall on the left. This soon improves into a good green path, rising imperceptibly into an inviting limestone and scrub amphitheatre.**

As the path fades keep faith with the wall to the top corner. Over the stile a firm track is joined. Follow this left to its demise on the brow. Chrome Hill, ahead and Parkhouse Hill, to the left make their presence known again. **Take the right-hand gate to cross a walled green way to another gate/stile, then a thin trod heads off across the pasture beneath a modest limestone scar and wall. From a stile at the end the slender defile of Dowel Dale appears below. A thin path winds down to join the narrow road.** Dowel Cave, just along to the left, has disclosed bones of birds and animals, evidence of occupation by Palaeolithic man perhaps 20,000 or more years ago.

Our way goes right along the road, rising between minor craggy walls to emerge onto a limestone plateau. As the road bends left up to a cattle-grid, Owl Hole is passed in a wooded enclosure on the right. **Opening out, verges now see us along the open road. Passing the farm drive to Greensides we rise higher, with High Edge up ahead, to arrive at a farm drive on the left. Head along this to quickly reach a fork at a cattle-grid.** This summit of the walk earns fresh views westwards into colourful upper Dove country backed by Axe Edge.

Parkhouse Hill from Chrome Hill

The opening up of a concession path traversing Chrome Hill has shed a different light on the options available here. Previously it would have been the norm to go via Booth Farm and on to Hollinsclough, but as Chrome Hill's jagged ridge makes its timely appearance, who could now resist the 'Dragon's Back'? As this is not a public right of way, it is imperative we don't stray from it and jeopardise its status.

Turn left off the drive, along the wallside and through further stiles on the gentle brow. Passing through an old wall - with Tor Rock just to the right - bear right, dropping steeply past a deep hole to find a stile at the foot of the fence on the left. Unfrequented country in front sees the side valley of Swallow Brook with its tree-lined stream and down-like flanks leading across to Hollins Hill and Hollinsclough.

40

The path heads along the bottom of the enclosure to pass through a stile in an old wall and fence. Here, just as the path's intentions were being doubted, a waymark sends it back up the slope, steeply left to soon ease out by a wall corner at the start of the ridge proper. Simply turn right and walk the crest to gain the summit, an exquisite limestone switchback known descriptively as the Dragon's Back.

Care is needed above steep declivities, initially on the south flank then later on the north. A natural little arch is passed just short of reaching the bare summit at about 1411ft/430m. The glorious views reach over much of this part of Peakland, some features of note including the Axe Edge skyline; a very dwarfed Parkhouse Hill leading the eye to the tree-lined Dove Valley and the parallel Manifold Valley; also well sited is Dowall Hall almost beneath our feet. Kinder Scout spreads its broad shoulders to the north, beyond the extensive but surprisingly well hidden quarries above Buxton.

Descent simply forges on down the grassier eastern ridge, down to a stile under a lone tree and then over a miniature dragon's back to meet the road into Dowel Dale. Cross the stile by the cattle-grid and turn right on the verge, beneath the shapely eminence of the Sugar Loaf. This rises fortress-like at the base of Parkhouse Hill, a diminutive gem whose lure should be rejected as there is no access: enjoying Chrome Hill is perhaps reasonable compensation. The road runs along its southern flank, now in the Dove Valley proper, becoming enclosed to meet the B5053 Longnor road at Glutton Bridge. The bridge itself, just along to the right, straddles the Dove and thus the Derbyshire-Staffordshire boundary. In amongst the few buildings is a former cheese factory that closed in the 1960s.

Go left past the phone box then quickly right along a back road. This continues on, more roughly after the Underhill Farm turning, through the fields to a solitary house. Here turn left and slant back up the field to a stile. The path splits but re-unites to climb a steep scrubby bank. Enjoy a further grand prospect of Chrome and Parkhouse Hills before they disappear from view.

Go left with the wall to a corner stile, then rise up onto the brow at the back of Hitter Hill. Earl Sterndale appears ahead just minutes away. Advance a little and take a stile on the right, then descend two fieldsides to return to the start at the rear of the pub.

LATHKILL HEAD

START *Monyash*   *Grid ref. SK 149665*

DISTANCE *5½ miles (or 4½ miles)*

ORDNANCE SURVEY MAPS
1:50,000
Landranger 119 - Buxton, Matlock & Dove Dale
1:25,000
Outdoor Leisure 24 - Peak District, White Peak

ACCESS *Start from the village centre. Car park on Chapel Street, just along from the central crossroads: other roadside parking. Served by bus from Buxton (not Sunday) and schoolday bus from Bakewell.*

An exciting dip into the upper reaches of a beautiful limestone dale.

S A windswept thousand feet up on the limestone plateau, Monyash was once a busy lead mining centre. It acquired a market charter in 1340, and a market cross still occupies the village green. Alongside are the welcoming 17th century *Bulls Head* and an equally tempting tearoom. There is also a shop/tearoom along the street past the church. St. Leonard's church dates back 800 years, but was restored in 1887. Fere Mere is the lone survivor of five clay-lined ponds for retaining precious water in these limestone uplands.

From the green head along to the church, and cross to the far side of the yard where a stile admits into a field. Head away, through a dip and maintain a straight line across a couple more fields. A farm lane is joined at a stile just short of the field corner. Stay on this to its demise. En route it improves, the final section being footway only to emerge into Fern Dale. This limestone and hawthorn pasture is a foreground to the craggy upper walls of Lathkill Dale. Look back, also, over the landscape of an archetypal limestone plateau.

42

Advance just a short way with the wall and take a stile in it, then on through the grassy hummocks of old lead workings crossing the head of Fern Dale. From the stile across, the path forks. The direct route goes straight on with the wall, keeping its company on one side or the other and finishing as an enclosed farm track to reach One Ash Grange. The longer route extends the walk and offers wider views, delaying the plunge into Lathkill Dale.

Slant up the field centre to a gap in the crumbling wall above, and continue across to a stile in the wall opposite. Far to the left is Over Haddon beyond Lathkill Dale, with Manners Wood behind and East Moor beyond. Cross to another gap in a crumbling wall and on to a stile just beyond, where another fork occurs. The left branch crosses the field to a stile then runs on the wallside to join the full route on the One Ash Grange drive.

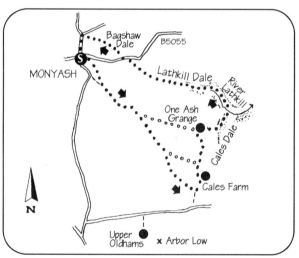

The slightly longer way gives a better look at upper Cales Dale. Slant right again to a stile in the far top corner, then cross a slim field to the next one. Similarly, head on again down to a stile in a wall overlooking Cales Dale. Cross it in the company of an old wall, and take a stile in the nearest corner above. Follow the left-hand wall away to join the Cales Farm drive. Go left towards the farm, but keep left at the fork outside it to head for One Ash Grange.

The drive drops down to negotiate Cales Dale again, now a deeper cleft brightened by limestone outcrops and hawthorn scrub. At a cattle-grid up the other side, the shorter route joins in. **Remain on this drive down to the farm, the lower section being a concession path which is less hassle than the public footpath.** Ahead, Lathkill Dale is brilliantly seen now around its junction with Cales Dale. Entering the farm the shortest route comes in from the left. **Turn right into the yard, but then veer left around the back of the buildings.**

Lathkill
Head
Cave

One Ash Grange was a grange of Roche Abbey in South Yorkshire, and an appropriate link with Monyash, which means 'many ash trees'. It consists of an immensely impressive range of buildings, and also has a camping barn offering inexpensive overnight accommodation. **We pass a set of stone feeder troughs and pig sties of novel design, and an intriguing grotto hewn from the rock. When the track forks keep straight on (right), passing between modern and traditional barns to a gap-stile at the end (watch the steep drop!).**

Descend the quickly forming hollow to suddenly be immersed in undergrowth amid limestone walls. The path drops quickly down into Cales Dale (again). Go left, a brief journey down this dry valley leading to a footbridge on the Lathkill. Just to the right is an old sheepwash, where fleeces could be washed at clipping time.

Joining the main path turn left through the resplendent limestone scenery of Lathkill Dale, with its oft-dry stream bed. Certainly a flow of water is not guaranteed, and in dry spells it can be some distance downstream before the Lathkill springs into life. Winter offers the best chance, at least as far as Holmes Groove, an old mining adit. **Passing a side valley guarded by a limestone tor, the dale becomes a deeper**

defile. On the left is Lathkill Head Cave. In suitable conditions it makes a fine sight when the stream emerges into daylight from this cavernous hole. Opposite, up to the right, Parson's Tor recalls the fate of Robert Lomas, a Monyash vicar who plummeted to meet his Maker here in 1776.

Now firmly in a dry valley, the path runs delightfully along the floor to a stile into mixed terrain. Before entering, look back down the limestone scarred edges of the dale. **The path runs through a ravine, decreasing in scale until emerging into a field. The green way remains obvious as it runs on to join the B5055 beneath the village.**

For the best finish go left just a few yards and cross to a gate/stile on the right below a barn. A footpath runs faintly along through little Bagshaw Dale, the shallow, uppermost continuation of Lathkill Dale. Stiles see us on through to join Horse Lane on the edge of the village. Along to the right is the well preserved village pinfold on the roadside. **Go left to climb back up into Monyash.** Going back to the 17th century the Quaker movement had strong influence hereabouts, and a humble old building on the right is a former Friends' Meeting House. There is a tiny burial ground at the back, and some remarkable fossilisation in the door lintel. On the left is a surviving Primitive Methodist Chapel of 1888.

Monyash

10

LATHKILL DALE & BRADFORD DALE

START Over Haddon   *Grid ref. SK 203664*

DISTANCE 6¾ miles

ORDNANCE SURVEY MAPS
1:50,000
Landranger 119 - Buxton, Matlock & Dove Dale
1:25,000
Outdoor Leisure 24 - Peak District, White Peak

ACCESS *Start from the village car park and toilets. Served by bus from Bakewell (not Sunday). An alternative start is Youlgreave, if coming by bus: there is only limited parking but Moor Lane car park west of the village (grid ref. 194644) is only just off-route.*

Delectable river scenery linking Bradford Dale and the foot of Lathkill Dale by way of the limestone plateau, with several villages featuring.

S   Over Haddon is an unassuming village in a glorious setting overlooking Lathkill Dale. The *Lathkil Hotel* (once the *Miners Arms*) on the edge of the village is a welcoming place, further enhanced by the view from its cosy bar. St. Anne's church dates from the late 19th century, and a Wesleyan Reform Chapel of 1861 stands near the pub. The village also has craft workshops and tearooms, and an English Nature information centre.

From the car park take the adjacent lane down past the church to the river at Lathkill Lodge. For now cross straight over on the clapper bridge (or dry ford) and a good track climbs the steep wooded bank. After a zigzag it emerges at the top into a field. Look back over the wooded dale to see the village spread along the hillside opposite.

Bear left across the field towards the farm buildings in the hollow, and a gate admits to the yard at Meadow Place Grange. The layout of this former monastic grange of Leicester Abbey is outstanding, with superior farm buildings ranged around a large courtyard.

Cross straight over to a stile and gate and up a short way between walls. Entering a field, rise up the wallside (past a fork) till it turns away, then slant up over the brow to a stile at the end. Look back to see the farm overtopped by the village, and also Manners Wood, East Moors, and Stanton in Peak under Stanton Moor. **Slant to the top corner and up again to a stile onto a road (Back Lane). Straight across, head down the field to pass through the wooded line of a narrow mineral rake and across to another road, the narrow Moor Lane.** Moor Lane car park is a few minutes up to the right.

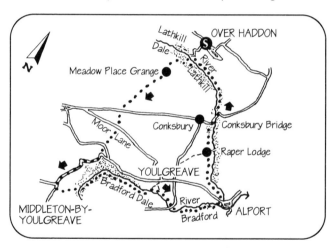

Once more cross over and down the fieldside, with several more stiles leading down to cross a further road. Drop down through trees and across to yet another road. Turn right along here, with a footway to assist and Bradford Dale on the left, to enter Middleton. Before reaching the village the gritstone mansion of Lomberdale Hall is passed. This was the home of Thomas Bateman, a tireless archaeologist who it seems excavated every burial site in the district, in a Victorian manner which today is seen as, at best, blundering. He died in 1861 and his tomb can be visited just ahead.

Middleton by Youlgreave - it likes to stress its individuality in a district of Middletons - is a quiet estate village with much interest in amongst its attractive cottages. Bateman's tomb is behind the former United Reform Chapel of 1826: simply turn along a short path on its near side, and the tomb sits just up the field-side in front. In the field across the road, grassy mounds and a few stones in the trees are all that remain of a castle: the name is remembered in Castle Farm. A well dated 1876 stands on the left approaching the centre, with at least two more nearby. Middleton Hall stands in spacious grounds up the side road.

At the central junction go ahead by the memorial garden and toilets, and just before the tiny St. Michael's church turn down Stinking Lane on the left. This quickly transforms into an enclosed way to descend into a wooded dell. Between substantial limestone scars it drops down into Bradford Dale. Here are scant ruins of a pump house, and the intact walls and compartments of what appears to be a sheepwash, complete with sunken section. The valley is normally dry at this stage. **Turn left on the well worn path downstream, between steep, wooded flanks and alongside lengths of the river Bradford adapted to store water. Maintain this course all the way down to Youlgreave.** When the trees are bare, the village is heralded in advance by the appearance of a long line of houses on the bank above.

On reaching a clapper-style footbridge change banks. The direct route turns downstream in contrastingly open pasture. To visit Youlgreave, turn up Holywell Lane past a little tearoom, entering the main street by way of the toilets and village hall. Directly opposite is the beautiful Old Hall dated 1656, while up behind it on Moor Lane is Old Hall Farm, bearing a 1630 datestone. **The heart of the village is just along to the right.**

Youlgreave - locally *Pommy* - was a lead mining centre, and today is an elongated village through which a narrow street struggles. Prime feature is the imposing 15th century tower of All Saints' church, parts of which date back to Norman times. Old monuments include a cross-legged knight over 700 years old; and that of Robert Gilbert, dating from 1492 it features him with his 7 sons, wife, 10 daughters, and the Virgin & Child. Numerous other features are also worthy of attention.

Other places of worship are a Wesleyan Methodist Chapel of 1807, a Wesleyan Reform Chapel of 1867 and a Primitive Methodist Chapel of 1895. Unusual village features are the water tank known as the

Fountain, which brought the first piped water to the village in 1829; adjacent is Thimble Hall, the tiniest cottage imaginable. Numerous shops still supply local needs in this none too 'touristy' village, while a choice of pubs offers the *Bulls Head, George* and *Farmyard Inn*. A youth hostel makes sympathetic use of the former Co-op.

The Fountain, Youlgreave

Leave by the way you entered, past the Wesleyan Reform Chapel, but turn sharp left down Brookleton, a footpath taking over at the bottom to drop back down to the riverbank.

With or without the diversion into Youlgreave, head downstream to reach a road. Cross straight over and a drive resumes downstream beneath limestone scars. The stream is crossed without noticing, as an arched packhorse bridge is passed on the other side. **The way continues though the path short-cuts the drive to stay with the river for a spell: when the drive turns off, stay on the riverbank beneath the sheer 70ft limestone face of Rhienstor. Beyond here the river is crossed and a drive leads up onto the road at Alport.**

Alongside, the Bradford is absorbed into the Lathkill. Across the bridge a cross-shaft is set into the wall, and a short detour is recommended down the side lane. Passing the attractive Monks Hall with its mullioned and transomed windows, the lane leads past a footbridge over the fast-flowing stream to an arched bridge on the Lathkill. This is a charming spot, neat cottages and a lively stream overlooked by a craggy, wooded bank: just downstream from the bridge, a waterwheel survives alongside an 18th century mill. Go left back up onto the main road, left again with Rock House opposite, and a notice discouraging 'vagabonds' on a barn wall (illustrated on page 3).

Cross the road and head upstream, separated from the river by a wall. A string of stiles lead past millponds on the river, to pass beneath Raper Lodge onto an old lane. Raper Lodge is an architecturally intriguing old building, while just down to the right an old packhorse bridge holds back a millpond. **Cross straight over the lane, and on a little further to join a road beneath Conksbury.** In the field opposite it is easy to discern the banks and ditches of a medieval village. **Turn right down to Conksbury Bridge.** This was first built as a packhorse bridge carrying the road from Bakewell to Youlgreave. Up-dale, the houses and pub at Over Haddon sit on the skyline.

Cross and turn upstream on a good path, which this time savours the river's company, and leads unfailingly back to Lathkill Lodge. Along the way, perhaps paralleling a dipper, we trace an unbroken line of weirs up the river: fish gather in the resulting pools. As the Lathkill is quite the purest of streams, the prized fishing rights are zealously protected. Just prior to Lathkill Lodge the river normally ends (or in our case begins) its dry spell by emerging from watercress beds at Bubbling Springs, the final yards usually being dry. **Turn back up the lane to finish.**

Conksbury Bridge

11

STANTON MOOR

START *Rowsley*   *Grid ref. SK 256658*

DISTANCE *6½ miles*

ORDNANCE SURVEY MAPS
1:50,000
Landranger 119 - Buxton, Matlock & Dove Dale
1:25,000
Outdoor Leisure 24 - Peak District, White Peak

ACCESS *Start from the village centre. There is a central car park. Served by Bakewell-Matlock buses and other less frequent services.*

An absorbing excursion to a gritstone island in the sky, to find heather and silver birch trees hiding an open air Bronze Age museum.

S Rowsley is a village of two halves, once Great and Little Rowsley. It is split by the river Derwent, the 15th century bridge having been much widened in the 1920s. Most interest is in the older, western half (Great Rowsley), including St. Katherine's church which boasts the impressive 1823 tomb of Lady Catherine Manners and a 9th century Anglo-Saxon cross-head. Also here are the school, a cross bearing an old roadsign, and the rich frontage of the up-market *Peacock Hotel*. This bears a 1652 datestone and was originally a dower house of Haddon Hall. The peacock features on the Manners' coat of arms.

The Post office/shop is on Church Lane, and across from the hotel is a well dated 1841. Down School Lane is Caudwells Mill, a working flour mill dating from 1875 which now incorporates craft workshops. East of the river is the *Grouse & Claret* pub with a camping/caravan site on the riverbank. The former station of the Midland Railway's Derby-Buxton Line was its terminus for some years. Rowsley is the last village on the Wye, which immediately downstream submits to the Derwent.

From the main road cross the bridge on the Derwent to the western half of the village, and turn left along School Lane. Past the school the road crosses the river Wye and turns sharp right. **Keep straight on along a private road.** High on the skyline ahead is Earl Grey's Tower on Stanton Moor, our objective. **The drive remains surfaced as it rises through Holly Wood to approach Stanton Woodhouse.**

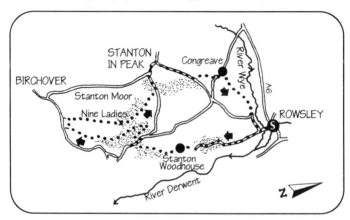

Emerging from the trees locate an iron kissing-gate part hidden in the hedge on the right. A part flagged path rises to join a track, going left through a gate to a hairpin bend of the drive. **Keep right on it to Stanton Woodhouse Farm.** The range of farm buildings here is quite superb, with the farmhouse itself hidden behind. On the left meanwhile is the old house of Stanton Woodhouse itself, a manor house dating back to Elizabethan times. Originally a shooting lodge for the Dukes of Rutland from Haddon Hall, we gain sufficient glimpse to ascertain its character and setting. Up above, meanwhile, the tower is looming larger!

Keep on to a gate at the end from where a green track rises through the field, up above Hillcar Wood to a gateway and old stile. All around is colourful country, and beyond the gateway bear left on a path rising to a gate. The now channelled path rises above the former Endcliffe Quarry to run down to join a narrow back road. Double back uphill and at the first chance take a green track rising left to the big quarry face it once served. This is a concession path on the Haddon Hall Estate: the right of way leaves the road further up.

At the quarry entrance stands a tall ruin. Go left of this to find a splendid path running on into the trees. A National Trust sign announcing Stanton Moor Edge is met at a sharp bend. Turn right with the main path, running a largely level course past another recolonised quarry face and lichen-covered low ruins. Towards the end (beyond another Haddon estate sign) the public path rises to join us from the right. This left the road at a stile just short of a quarry to climb the field to a stile into the wood just beneath our path.

The path curves round to rise along the edge of the wood. After being enveloped by trees at the woodtop, the heather of Stanton Moor makes its first showing to the right. A stile in the adjacent fence gives access, but our ambling route is far better, remaining on the path outside the fence to quickly reach the tower. Known as Earl Grey's Tower, it was built in 1832 by the Thornhill family of Stanton to mark the passing of the Reform Bill (and named after the then Prime Minister). It is a tall, sturdy four-square structure clearly in good condition, but nevertheless the doorway has been filled in. A flight of stone steps lead up to it from the wood.

Resist another stile onto the moor and keep on the woodtop path, known as Dukes Drive. Initially through trees, it soon leaves them at a corner. Not initially obvious but easily identified is the boulder known as the Cat Stone with its carved jugholds. The fence remains for company as we now savour the heathery delights of Stanton Moor, and outstanding views with the edge dropping away beneath us. Just down the Derwent Valley is Matlock, with the shell of Riber Castle on the skyline beyond. A boundary stone by the fence is inscribed *DR 1815*. Remain on this delectable path past occasional outcrops to swing round a corner and on to a stile and NT sign at a large boulder.

A labyrinth of paths make for this stile. Cross it and take the level path contouring to the left, joining a broad path rising from the left. Turn up this to quickly find a major path crossroads. Though our route is straight ahead, it is worth going left for a couple of minutes to inspect, and possibly surmount, the Cork Stone, a remarkable isolated rock complete with carved jugholds and iron handles.

Keep straight on for a glorious half mile to the Nine Ladies Stone Circle. Stanton Moor is awash with scheduled ancient monuments, dozens of tumuli and some lesser circles. En route we pass several of these distinctive funerary remains, including a circular barrow on the right, plum on the path; and then before the trees a circular enclosure on the left with its kerbed bank, fully 25 yards in diameter and probably the largest on the moor. **Scattered trees are entered to find the stone circle in a clearing straight in front.** All in their rightful place, the Nine Ladies are of Bronze Age origin, somewhere between 3500-4000 years old. The modest circle is 10 yards in diameter, and was built as a burial mound (large barrow), thus originally having an earth covered mound (illustrated on page 8). Just to the west is the simple and recently damaged King's Stone.

Resume on the main path, which runs on across the moor and through light woodland to a stile where we leave the site. Passing a stone water tank the broad path quickly leaves the moor and runs on through a couple of fields to join a narrow road. Turn left to drop down through the woods into Stanton in Peak.

Stanton is a charming village straggling up a steep road. On the right is a Wesleyan Reform Chapel of 1829, followed by numerous pleasing corners secreting neat cottages. At the junction is an enclosed green, while unseen to the left is the large Stanton Hall of the Thornhill family. Open to all is the church of the Holy Trinity, built in 1839 by the Thornhills. Though of modest proportions, certainly internally, the spire flatters itself as typical of the area. Inside is a fine bronze Italian holy water stoup dated 1596 and a pair of Jacobean chairs dated 1655 and 1669.

Further down the street are a Post office/shop and the unassuming *Flying Childers* pub, named after a racehorse of the Duke of Devonshire. Opposite is a fine house known as Holly House, of particular interest for its numerous blocked up windows, probably to combat the effects of a once notorious 'window tax'.

Leave Stanton by turning right at the junction along the Rowsley road above the graveyard and school. The half-mile walk along this quiet road is a delight in itself, for it offers beautiful views up the valley of the Wye. Centrepiece of this fair scene is the grand mansion of Haddon Hall in its fine grounds (see the companion book *Central Peak*), with Bakewell beyond.

Just after a lone cottage (Beighton House) take a stile on the left. Fifty yards before this, an unusual Victorian feature is the Stand, a semi-circular stone viewing platform complete with stone benches for an entire group to eat their packed lunch in comfort. **From the stile slant down to a gap-stile just above a gate, then on by a line of trees to a stile at the end. Continue along the fieldside to a stile (Rowsley appears ahead) onto a narrow climbing road. Turn down through the steep zigzags of the hamlet of Congreave.**

Part way down take a green way on the right above a barn, quickly debouching into a field. A thin path crosses it, dropping down to a gate beneath a small wood. Briefly rising through the trees, emerge to contour across the field to a line of trees. Up above is the prominent wooded knoll of Peak Tor. **Go left on an old green way dropping down by the trees.** Beneath us the river Wye winds cheerily through the pastures of its final mile (having itself only just absorbed the waters of the Lathkill). A ditch and bank are shadowed by the trees alongside the path, and as our way leaves them at the bottom, the very distinct ditch and bank can be seen encircling the slope of this knoll, suggestive of a deer park boundary.

The track slants down above the Wye, running on to a stile/gate onto a back road just by the river. Go straight ahead on this past sports fields to rejoin the outward route on the edge of the village.

Earl Grey's Tower, Stanton Moor

12

LATHKILL DALE

START Youlgreave   Grid ref. SK 194644

DISTANCE 5¼ miles

ORDNANCE SURVEY MAPS
1:50,000
Landranger 119 - Buxton, Matlock & Dove Dale
1:25,000
Outdoor Leisure 24 - Peak District, White Peak

ACCESS Start from the National Park's Moor Lane car park a mile west of the village. Youlgreave is served by bus from Bakewell (not Sunday). An alternative start is Over Haddon (see WALK 10).

A captivating walk through the heart of Lathkill Dale, which '...will transport you to the very threshold of Arcady' (W. A. Poucher, 1966)

🅢 **From the car park turn right down the road, descending for a few minutes with sweeping views ahead. When it levels out, a footpath crosses it. Take the stile/gate on the left and cross to the line of trees. A path runs through the wooded confines of Long Rake and across a field onto another road (Back Lane). Cross straight over and bear right, aiming for Over Haddon which appears on the hillside across unseen Lathkill Dale. Maintain this course on the faint path until Meadow Place Grange appears in front.**

Descend to the wall corner above it and drop down into the yard. The layout of this former grange of Leicester Abbey is outstanding, with superior farm buildings ranged around a large courtyard. **Go straight across to pass between stables and barn opposite, and out into the field behind. Cross and bear right to a corner gate.** The deep trough of Lathkill Dale now reveals itself, though the tree cover is such that little is really seen: Over Haddon is just across now. **Through the**

gate a cart track descends the wood, zigzagging down to the valley floor at the isolated Lathkill Lodge. Cross by clapper bridge or ford. The Lathkill is regularly dry at this point, though it does appear only yards downstream at Bubbling Springs. Over Haddon is just a few minutes up the lane climbing steeply away (see page 46).

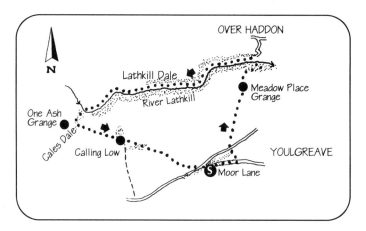

Turn up between the buildings but then pass behind the barns at Sough Mill on the left to a gate. Here we enter the Lathkill Dale National Nature Reserve, a highly valued tract of limestone grassland and woodland. Numerous signs waylay us, including a notice proclaiming that on the Thursday of Easter week a toll of one penny is chargeable: this underlines the fact that the ensuing mile and a half is on a concession path, not a public footpath. It is the only path through this part of the reserve, so please stay on it as numerous rare plant species find refuge in the native ash woodlands. In addition, it can be closed for shooting on some Wednesdays from October to January.

A broad track heads up-dale, largely through densely wooded country. At once we pass a reedy millpond, and quickly reach the site of the Mandale lead mine. Back in the 19th century the now forlorn ruin housed a Cornish-type beam engine, and at the side was a waterwheel 35ft in diameter: a crucial and never-ending task was that of pumping water from the mine below. The 100ft shaft has wisely been capped.

A little upstream are the stone supports of an aqueduct, built in 1840 to carry water from further up the dale. It supplied the waterwheel by way of a now dry watercourse up to the right. **Simply forge on the track, one section being on a raised walkway to escape occasional flooding.** Beyond here are the distinctive hollows and mounds of former lead workings: the area was worked over many centuries, back to when the valley was in the hands of monastic granges.

Another dam is passed, and as the cart track ends we emerge into the open at the foot of a side valley leading up to Haddon Grove. At this point we are back on a public footpath. Just in front are the scant remains of Carter's Mill, a small cornmill: a couple of millstones lie by the path. **The clear path resumes up the valley, passing another weir and millpond.** The clarity of the pool typifies the purity of the Lathkill, said to be unrivalled thanks to its entire existence being in limestone country.

Visible ahead and quickly reached are Lathkill Falls. If anywhere merits a break it is at this low waterfall. The stream tumbles over an apron of tufa, the result of limestone deposits (calcium carbonate) carried in the pure, lime-rich waters. To the right, meanwhile, gleaming limestone scars tower above. **The smashing walk advances further along the dale floor to arrive at a footbridge.**

Unless incorporating WALK 9, which continues up-dale to Monyash, then this is the turning point. **Cross the bridge and a path runs along the side valley of Cales Dale, very quickly reaching a fork. Cross the stile on the left and a flight of stone steps demands a stiff pull up the bank.** At the top pause to savour the view back over the upper flanks of Lathkill Dale. **From the kissing-gate head on up the fields, several of these gates featuring as we rise on a sometimes faint path towards the farm buildings of Calling Low, another monastic grange.**

The diverted footpath avoids the farm, and is clearly marked as it rises left of the buildings, through plots of woodland and out the other side. Bear right to a gate, then cross the large field to the far corner, just short of the end of Low Moor Plantation. From the stile the path crosses to the end of the wood, on to a stile and then heads away across a vast field, slanting down to a stile with the wooded Bee Low over to the left. From a stile just beyond, cross to the far corner of the field where a stile admits onto a road junction. The start is just along the side road in front, passing over the deep trough of Long Rake to finish.

(13)

RAIL TRAILS

START *Parsley Hay*   *Grid ref. SK 147636*

DISTANCE *6½ miles*

ORDNANCE SURVEY MAPS
1:50,000
Landranger 119 - Buxton, Matlock & Dove Dale
1:25,000
Outdoor Leisure 24 - Peak District, White Peak

ACCESS *Start from the National Park's Parsley Hay car park on the A515 north-east of Hartington. Leek-Bakewell buses on Mondays and Summer Sunday/BH Monday Bakewell-Buxton buses are among the infrequent services. Alternative starts are trail-side car parks at Friden and Hartington station.*

An easy walk on old railways, linking the long established High Peak and Tissington Trails. Light footwear very definitely adequate.

❺ At Parsley Hay Wharf the London & North Western Railway's Ashbourne-Buxton line met the Cromford & High Peak Railway. Opened in 1899, the former had stations at Thorpe, Tissington, Alsop en le Dale and Hartington: all are visited in one or other of these walks. The CHPR, later absorbed by the LNWR, features in greater detail in WALK 19. The name wharf, incidentally, was applied to the string of small stations on the CHPR, in deference to its canal connections.

This walk has a special significance as in 1967 our chosen sections were in each case last to close; i.e. Parsley Hay to Friden and Parsley Hay to Hartington. The National Park and County Council enterprisingly purchased the lines which by 1972 were 'open for business' again - or rather leisure use. With a picnic site and cycle hire, Parsley Hay is a popular base for excursions on foot or saddle onto both trails.

Join the old railway line and turn left (south). After crossing the side road it almost immediately reaches a fork. This is the junction of the two lines, and the point to which we shall return through the deep rock cutting ahead. Note the direction stone set into the ground.

Bear left on the High Peak Trail, which remains our course for a good couple of miles as far as the brickworks at Friden. En route we pass through Derbyshire Wildlife Trust's Blake Moor nature reserve; while under the main road with its curious alignment note the stone bearing the crest of the CHPR, the dominant name being that of Josias Jessop, the line's engineer. Emerging from the cutting beyond this the way remains unenclosed, offering pleasant views. A couple of tracks are crossed before passing Brundcliffe Farm and rounding the corner to the brickworks, which appear well in advance.

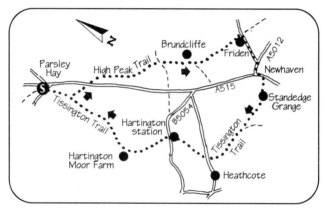

On crossing the road at the end of the Friden works, leave the line and follow the trail car park drive down onto the road. The massive brickworks have long since absorbed the farm of Friden Grange. The area was first worked over a century ago as local pits revealed a useful source of silica sand in amongst the limestone: specialised heat-resistant bricks for ovens and kilns are the result. **Turn left along the front of the brickworks for a quarter-mile to the A5012 junction alongside Friden Pit. Go briefly right to the grassy triangle.** Here stands a restaurant appropriately named *Carriages*. **Bear left onto the A515 Ashbourne-Buxton road, crossing it and almost at once taking a stile by a gate on the right.** Just yards further is the bleak sight of a closed pub, though perhaps it will be back in business some day.

Pass along to the far end of Newhaven House farm buildings, and through the gateway rise left up the field to a stile. Cross to another, then a string of stiles lead past the farm at Stanedge Grange. Join a track leading on to the far end, using a gap in Horseshoe Plantation. Here the track fades. The Tissington Trail sweeps along beneath us, with a fine prospect westwards past Biggin, with its church tower prominent. **Slant right, using gap-stiles in two intervening walls to gain the railside wall. A stile admits onto the line, and all that remains is to turn right for three miles of trail-blazing back to the start.**

Features en route include some splendid views left, looking back to Ecton and Wetton Hills beyond Hartington. A picnic site at Ruby Wood (planted to mark the 40th anniversary of the National Park in 1991) and a vast disused quarry are passed before arriving at Hartington station, with car park, picnic tables and a preserved signal box which acts as a seasonal information point. Further on, Hartington Moor Farm is passed before a high embankment leads on through Derbyshire Wildlife Trust's Parsley Hay nature reserve to the big 'V' of the rock cutting just short of the rail junction, and thus the end.

Parsley Hay is also well sited for a look at Arbor Low, the finest archaeological feature in the Peak, dubbed 'Stonehenge of the North'. It is sited along the Youlgreave road, being under a mile away on foot: cars can be parked at the farm there (Upper Oldhams), for a fee. Arbor Low is a circular henge dating back more than 3500 years. Of national importance, it features a set of now-recumbent limestone rocks surrounded by a bank and deep ditch.

*Signal box,
Hartington station*

14

GRATTON DALE

START Friden   Grid ref. SK 171607

DISTANCE 7½ miles

ORDNANCE SURVEY MAPS
1:50,000
Landranger 119 - Buxton, Matlock & Dove Dale
1:25,000
Outdoor Leisure 24 - Peak District, White Peak

ACCESS Start from the National Park's Friden car park on the High Peak Trail, off the A5012 at Newhaven. Served by Bakewell-Buxton Summer Sunday/BH Monday buses and other occasional services.

A walk into some lesser known dales, the simple lines of Long Dale contrasting with the livelier Gratton Dale. Though using the High Peak Trail as a convenient start point, this walk doesn't set foot on it.

⑤ **Return to the road opposite the large brickworks (see page 60). Turn right, under the railway and down towards a dip formed by a dry valley. Before the bottom of the road a path slips down to the right to a bridle-gate sending an old walled way off. Not only is the right of way omitted from the map, but the walled way itself is missing! This runs along the dry valley floor, emerging from walls between the Bolderstone plantations and on to a narrower section.**

Leaving the trees behind, Long Dale opens out. The bridleway strictly climbs the brow on the left to run along to a gate, from where a green track slants back down to the valley floor at a wall junction and bridle-gate. The natural line, however, is the green path follow-ing the wall through the valley bottom. Delectably easy strides lead through the peaceful charms of this archetypal dry limestone dale, with downland-type slopes, parts of which are within Long Dale

National Nature Reserve for the quality of the limestone grasslands. **This happy stride leads on to a T-junction of bridleways and dales. Turn left to enter Gratton Dale, at once clearly a very different beast.**

A thin path runs beneath occasional limestone outcrops. Much of the scrubby flanks was cleared in 1996 to encourage flowers and allow grazing. **Part way down a track forms, more substantial outcrops appear above, and a stream usually gurgles into life. At the end the way opens into a field by a restored limekiln. The track runs down to a narrow road by the phone box at Dale End, hub of Gratton parish.**

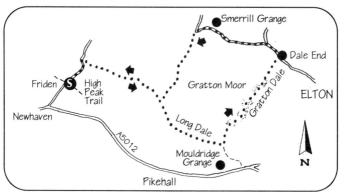

Go left on the road, quickly turning left at a fork where a slimmer back road climbs away. The building on the left was once a cheese factory. **At the top the road runs by Smerrill Grange Farm.** Down to the right, noteworthy limestone outcrops fringe the side valley of Rowlow Brook backed by Youlgreave and its massive church tower, while in the immediate foreground, before the farm, the grassy mounds of a medieval village can be clearly discerned. **Dropping to a sharp bend, leave the road for an enclosed bridleway on the left. This runs as a narrow, leafy way to emerge into a field.**

A firm farm track is joined, leading up the wallside for some way. At the top it becomes briefly enclosed to leave by the top left gate. As the track falters, keep to the left-hand wall. The character of the low walls we pass suggests these rows of big rocks are of some antiquity. **A gateway at the end leaves us overlooking Long Dale again. All that remains is to bear right along the bank top, dropping down at the end to rejoin the outward route and so retrace steps back to Friden.**

15

ROYSTONE GRANGE & PARWICH

START *Minninglow*   *Grid ref. SK 194581*

DISTANCE *7½ miles (or 3½ or 5¾ miles)*

ORDNANCE SURVEY MAPS
1:50,000
Landranger 119 - Buxton, Matlock & Dove Dale
1:25,000
Outdoor Leisure 24 - Peak District, White Peak

ACCESS *Start from the National Park's Minninglow High Peak Trail car park a good half-mile off the A5012 at Pikehall. An alternative start is Parwich (reasonable parking) with infrequent buses from Ashbourne.*

A gentle ramble based on the innovative Roystone Grange archaeological trail, with an optional extension midway to the attractive village of Parwich. Trail leaflet available at National Park centres.

❺ **The car park actually sits on the High Peak Trail: from the far end leave and immediately cross a narrow road to get on the trail proper.** For a note on this former railway, now the High Peak Trail, please refer to WALK 19. **The trail chugs off, a grand striding start with immediate interest as it crosses a high embankment.** This stone supported structure was built in the 1820s, with another near identical one soon to come. Ahead is the stubbly top of Minninglow itself, while below us is the farm of Minninglow Grange.

Passing an old quarry the line swings round to run on to the second embankment. Alongside is a larger quarry, with the remains of a crane and sections of track from its siding still in place. Across the embankment is a well preserved limekiln. **Just beyond, a track crosses the**

trail. **Here we leave it, but first advance a few yards to see a former brick kiln.** Local deposits of silica sand went to make fire-bricks, capable of withstanding the intense heat of furnaces. Large modern works exist nearby at Friden (WALK 14) and Harborough (WALK 20).

Back at the track, take a gate/stile above and follow it away, becoming a better green way as it progresses. This is Minninglow Lane, becoming Gallowlow Lane, an historic track that has seen use down many centuries. The walls added at such a respectable width further confirm the route's importance. **Leave at a stile on the right before a brow: at this point Minninglow is at its nearest, directly above us.** Minninglow is the largest chambered tomb in the Peak, and excavations revealed several burial chambers thought to be from the New Stone Age, perhaps 5000 years old.

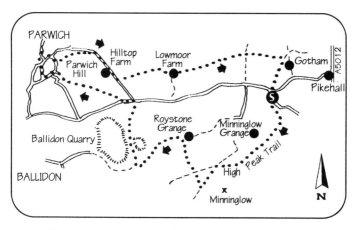

Descend past a little mere to the railway tunnel arch, and continue straight down. Ahead meanwhile, is Roystone Grange, still presenting a monastic type layout. Look up to the right to see a stone hut with a curved roof: this is a former explosives store for the quarry. **Before a second gateway our way is deflected over the wall by a stile onto a less favourable track than the green one we left. Descend this to a gateway.** This next field is the site of a 16th-18th century farm that existed between medieval times and the present. **Continue on to a stile in the wall, then slant left to another to join the unclassified road through the valley.**

Just yards to the right is Roystone Grange, the oldest buildings dating back only to the 18th century, though no doubt incorporating stonework of its predecessor. Just beyond the present farm is the site of a Roman manor house. The shortest return goes through the grange and remains on this old road to emerge onto Parwich Lane, a few minutes short of the start. **Go left on the rough road to be faced by a chapel-like building: enter its enclosure to see more.** The building is a 19th century pump house, in which a water cooled engine pumped compressed air to drive quarry drills up by the railway. Mossy stones to the right form the base of the monastic grange hall and barn. The Cistercian grange of Garendon Abbey in Leicestershire ran vast sheep pastures from which wool was exported all over Europe.

Back on the road head down the floor of this dry valley, sandwiched between some steep crags on the right and spectacular dolomitic limestone outcrops on the left. In the right lighting it is possible to detect, on the grassy slopes just past here, cultivation terraces from when Romans farmed the valley. **At the first opportunity leave at a guidepost, through a gate on the right where a side valley enters.**

Minninglow from the railside limekiln

The devastation of Ballidon's mushrooming quarry is upon us. A new section in view is nothing compared to what soon appears. **The right of way is well preserved by bizarrely crossing a bridge over the quarry link to its modern extension.** The awesome scale of workings begs the question 'how much Peak District will remain?'. **Continuing, within seconds it is all behind us.** Odd indeed that such an immense operation could impinge on our walk for a matter of seconds only! **The track runs along the dry valley floor to split beneath an old limekiln. The branch left rises by a wall to emerge at a road junction.** To omit Parwich take the road heading away, and within minutes paths leave from either side: take that to the right and pick up the main directions.

For Parwich, turn left just as far as the brow, and take a stile on the right. Slant down to a corner stile, on again to the same, then down the wallside. Ahead are big views to rolling country; modern field patterns have left an island barn isolated over to our left. Part way down a stile transfers us across, then cross to a stile in the wall ahead. From the next stile cross to the far corner alongside a dewpond. Advance to the wall corner ahead, to stand on the edge of the steeper slopes of Parwich Hill, with part of the village visible below.

Slant right, down the increasingly scrubby bank on a clear path that forms: it is worth locating as the scrub soon becomes denser. The path becomes clearer as it works down the bank to emerge from undergrowth alongside a house. Here is a sudden bird's-eye view over the village. Join the drive to run down through the highest houses, and down in the village proper bear right at a couple of junctions to run along the rear of the church to a small green. The main green and the pub are just to the left.

A homespun sign announces 'twinned with Abersoch', but Parwich is a charming place in its own right. Being off the beaten tourist track is of great benefit to the peaceful environs of the green, where a walled pond delays the stream, looking across to pub, church and an attractive three-storey cottage alongside. St. Peter's church dates from 1874 with some Norman remains, while the *Sycamore Inn* tempts with its range of food and drink. An endearing feature is the network of lanes delving into hidden corners: no simple main street here! Other features are noted as we move off.

Leave by the streamside track up the side of the green and continue on a footway in the stream's company, emerging onto a back road. Go left, passing the Wesleyan Methodist Chapel of 1845, then turn right up a narrow back lane and down past the school. Go right, and at the village shop turn left up the Newhaven road. This climbs to a junction in front of the hall. Parwich Hall dates from 1747, and boasts an elegant three-storey red brick front. A short-cut path climbs to the right branch, which follow uphill.

On the brow take a stile/gate on the left and rise to the field top, alongside the wood. From the stile climb a colourful pasture of scrub and limestone, and continue the slant up an easing slope. As with the descent to the village, locate an initially faint but well defined embanked path. To the left are grand rolling views, almost every field displaying evidence of medieval ridge and furrow ploughing. **The path curves gently up through modest scrub and then runs more easily and clearly along the lengthy pasture, only fading just short of the far end where a gate/gap-stile take us onto a road. Turn right for ten minutes, rising past Hilltop Farm and onto the brow.**

With stiles on either side, take that on the left. Here the shorter route from Ballidon Quarry joins in. **Head up the fieldside and 50 yards along to a stile, and resume over the brow past a barn.** Minninglow is prominent on the skyline over to the right; the line of the High Peak Trail can be traced beneath it; while in front are the dolomitic limestone outcrops of Roystone Rocks. **Dropping down after the corner, Lowmoor Farm is revealed in its side valley, with a lagoon and former quarry to its left.**

Descend to a stile in the corner then slant down to the farm, a stile admitting to the track in front. Cross and go left of the buildings to a stile in the corner behind, admitting onto a firm track. Climb away on this between trees, at the top advancing straight on to a stile, right of the gate. Continue through the field to the end of the T-shaped Lowmoor Plantation ahead. Cross straight over to the left-hand of two gates, and resume along the wallside. Maintain this course, passing through a stand of huddled beech. Down to the left, only the grassy embankment remains of a small dam associated with lead mining days.

A corner stile signals a sudden welcome transformation as we enter a series of grassy sheep pastures interrupted only by low crumbling walls. Maintain a line bearing slightly left to find a facing stile in an intact wall. Follow the wall away to enter a rough walled lane. This is Cobblersnook Lane, a continuation of the historic Minninglow Lane. **Cross and resume, from the next stile slanting up to the right of the trees. Head on through another, in line, to a gap in the strip woodland of Gotham Plantation. Pass through and descend the wallside, with the High Peak Trail appearing in front.** The bend just to the left is the famous Gotham Curve, the most acute on any line in the country: even modern-day cyclists slow down for it!

In the corner a stile alongside a small old quarry admits onto the line. Gotham Granges farms are below and up to the left. Turn right for the final few minutes through the trees of Chapel Planation, bridging the road to re-enter the car park.

16

HARTHILL MOOR

START *Elton*   *Grid ref. SK 222609*

DISTANCE *7 miles*

ORDNANCE SURVEY MAPS
1:50,000
Landranger 119 - Buxton, Matlock & Dove Dale
1:25,000
Outdoor Leisure 24 - Peak District, White Peak

ACCESS *Start from the village centre. Though parking is limited on the narrow main street, further east it broadens considerably and there is ample space on the north side. Alternative starts are Birchover and Winster. Served by Bakewell-Matlock buses.*

An absorbing ramble through idyllic countryside, the environs of Harthill Moor offering an extraordinary range of gritstone outcrops in addition to three interesting villages.

S Elton is a street village perched on a shelf where limestone and gritstone meet. All Saints' church was rebuilt in 1812 following a collapse of the tower. The village hall was originally a Wesleyan Methodist Chapel of 1831, and there is a Primitive Methodist Chapel of 1843 just beyond. The Old Hall bears a 1668 datestone, and is now a youth hostel. Also centrally placed is the *Duke of York* pub.

Head west along the main street. After the church turn down Well Street, at the first chance go left on a driveway. At the facing gate go into the field, left a few yards to the hedge and descend to a stile at the bottom. The path ahead can be traced through the fields up to the right. So, bear right to another stile then slant up the colourful fields through old walls, stiles and occasional hawthorn, to a corner stile onto a back road, Cross Lane.

Across, a path runs through undergrowth into a field. Rise up the wallside and advance to the brow. The view ahead opens out with Over Haddon above Lathkill Dale, backed by Longstone Edge on the skyline. **Advance to a fence-stile and straight on to join Cliff Farm drive. Cross straight over and down to a stile, then down the fields towards a plantation. Pass round to its left, and from a gateway head down another field.** Up to the right Harthill Moor Farm sits atop a steep grassy bank that held an Iron Age hillfort known as Castle Ring.

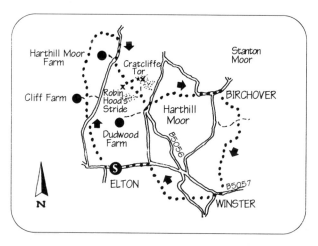

From the stile at the bottom descend again to reach a path crossroads at a small gate. Pass through and take the path contouring across to enter a wood. Youlgreave is briefly glimpsed spread across the slopes to the left. **The path curves delightfully round the wood and back onto Cliff Lane. Turn uphill, soon reaching the drive to Harthill Moor Farm, by which time the tors of Robin Hood's Stride loom ahead.**

From a stile opposite the farm drive slant across two fields to gain the open country of Robin Hood's Stride. Scrambling opportunities hide easier routes onto the rocks, where two tors known as the Inaccessible Pinnacle and Weasel Pinnacle dominate the scene. From the crest look out over the environs of Harthill Moor, with Nine Stones circle, comprising of four tall surviving stones, a couple of fields to the north. Further north are Youlgreave, Lathkill Dale and Over Haddon; east is Stanton Moor with East Moor slotting in beyond the Derwent Valley.

Robin Hood's improbable stride is also known as Mock Beggar's Hall, as from Elton it resembles a house with the pinnacles as chimneys. Our splendid green track here is on the line of the ancient Portway, a major route across the White Peak, possibly Bronze Age in origin and later adapted by Roman and Saxon travellers.

Weasel Pinnacle, Robin Hood's Stride

Before leaving, take a detour to Cratcliffe Tor. This short cul-de-sac path heads off left (east) through the old wall immediately after entering the site. It crosses a field to a stile into more bracken-clad, bouldery country. Much more awaits, so young 'uns should not go unrestrained. **Slanting up to the right gains the projecting gritstone plinth atop the buttress of Cratcliffe Tor, a stupendous moment. Slanting down to the right from the stile, the base of the cliffs conceals the Hermit's Cave, located behind a pair of ancient yews.** A crucifix is carved on the wall and there is a hole for a lamp. It was probably in use in medieval times, when the hermit's life was relatively popular, and the Portway would still have been a regular thoroughfare.

Back on the Portway under Robin Hood's Stride, resume as it becomes briefly enclosed beneath a wood to a gate/stile into a field. Pause to look back up at the Stride before moving off. **The path runs down to join the Cratcliffe Cottage drive.** This isolated cottage boasts an enviable location directly under the towering cliff. **The drive runs down onto a farm drive at a junction with the B5056 (A524 on some older maps).** While descending, the hollowed Portway is parallel just to the right. For a quick return to Elton, turn up the tiny side road climbing away.

Go left for 150 yards on the main road, and take a stile on the right. This comes just after passing an old milestone inscribed *Bakewell 5 miles, Ashbourn (sic) 12 miles.* **Climb the scrubby bank to a stile at the top, joining a broader path.** Pause to look back over the delights of the last section, now seen in a wider setting. **Go left on the path, which runs beneath woodland before being gradually transformed into an access road rising to the edge of Birchover.**

Before the top, the bouldery wood on the left harbours Rowtor Rocks. Within small compass are mystical delights with romanticised druidical legends attached. Gritstone caves, seats and stairways were carved to form a retreat for the local vicar, Thomas Eyre, who died in 1717. **Back up onto the road, meanwhile, we emerge alongside the handily placed and aptly named *Druid Inn.*** Long ago the pub supplied a guide to show people round the rocks.

On the right is the church of St. Michael & All Angels, and next door is the former school with its bell still in place. **Advance along the street to the junction with Uppertown Lane.** Features passed include another pub, the *Red Lion*, toilets and a shop. At the junction is a Primitive Methodist Chapel of 1867, and a little beyond, a pinfold.

Yards after the old Wesleyan Reform Church on the left, take a track between houses on the right to enter a yard. At the far end a gate/ stile send us off across the field. Passing through a line of trees advance to a stile at the very end. Cross the next field to a stile ahead, midway along the wall. Turn right along the fieldside to a gate/stile onto Clough Lane, a rough road.

Cross straight over and head away along a track. As Birchover disappears behind, Winster and Elton appear ahead. A path takes over to reach the top of a scrubby bank, with Winster facing us across the valley, its houses straggling up the hillside. Indeed, our path thereto can be discerned much of the way.

The path slants down the bank to a stile below, then across to join another path through a hedge. This runs pleasantly down to the left to the bottom of the virtually dry valley. A slim causey crosses the bottom, and newly installed flagstones lead across, interlinking with original causeyed path that is slowly finding its way back to the surface. The clear path rises to join an access track from a wildlife pond, and this rises as Woodhouse Lane onto Winster's main street.

Winster was a busy place at the height of 18th century lead mining, and its focal point is another reminder of more important times, its centuries-old market hall. It was the National Trust's first Derbyshire acquisition in 1906, and the old arches have been bricked up to afford greater stability: it now houses an information display (open summer weekends). The church of St. John the Baptist was restored in the 19th century, and there is a Wesleyan Reform Chapel of 1852.

Lining the main street are numerous buildings of stature, none more so than the elegant Georgian Winster Hall. There are also lots of nooks and crannies scattered up the slopes behind, where old miners' cottages predominate. Winster has shops, a Post office, toilets, and the *Bowling Green* pub. At the top of the village, by an area known as the Flat, is another pub, the *Miners Standard*: it bears a 1653 datestone and is named from the dish used by miners to weigh a measure of ore.

At the junction at the end turn up West Bank, then sharp right along a footway into the churchyard. Pass along the top to a stile into attractive grounds. A path heads away, behind a house and on to the end. Passing through a strip of woodland the way runs on to emerge onto the B5056. To the right Robin Hood's Stride, Cratcliffe Tor and Stanton Moor are upstanding.

Cross straight over and head away, a faint path running on through stiles in crumbling walls. Further, it crosses a large field to the far right corner, and a cross-roads of ways. Cross the farm drive and go right along the lesser lane. This splendid byway is said to be a further section of the Portway. **It broadens to join the road just east of Elton. Go left to finish.**

Rowtor Rocks, Birchover

17

BONSALL & OKER

START *Darley Bridge*   *Grid ref. SK 270620*

DISTANCE *5¾ miles*

ORDNANCE SURVEY MAPS
1:50,000
Landranger 119 - Buxton, Matlock & Dove Dale
1:25,000
Outdoor Leisure 24 - Peak District, White Peak

ACCESS *Start from the village of South Darley, or Darley Bridge on maps. There is a little parking immediately over the bridge on Oker Lane, and roadside parking up the hill from the pub. Served by Matlock-Bakewell buses.*

An enjoyable leg-stretcher finding both interest and charm in the limestone and lead mining country on the edge of the National Park.

S The settlement of South Darley is perhaps better known as Darley Bridge. The bridge itself spans the Derwent in two arches, and dates back to the 15th century. The nucleus of the old village is alongside the bridge, with a pub - the *Three Stags Heads* (1736 datestone) - and cottages and a Post office. There is another pub *(Square & Compass)* across the bridge, while the rest of the village straggles up the hill towards Wensley, and includes the church of St. Mary the Virgin.

From the bridge walk through the village (Winster road) to the *Three Stags Heads* and up the road with its convenient footway. At the junction opposite the church (Cross Green), cross to the school and head up a snicket between village hall and school. This runs on as a field-path to join a road. To the left rises the modest but colourful Oker Hill. Cross straight over (entering the National Park) and along a short way to enter a field. Head down to a corner stile, slant right

to a gap in the hedge, and on to find a stile in the corner below. Between craggy limestone knolls we emerge into **Wensley Dale.** Not on the scale or grandeur of its Yorkshire namesake, this is nevertheless a lovely little valley. The village of Wensley is just up to the right.

Advance to a path crossroads and go straight across, a faint path slanting up the brow and rising to the far top corner, finding a stile above the re-entrant of Northern Dale. This is an old lead mining area, and from here-on regular evidence is seen in the form of covered shafts and grassy mounds. Over to the left is the shell of Riber Castle on the hilltop above Matlock.

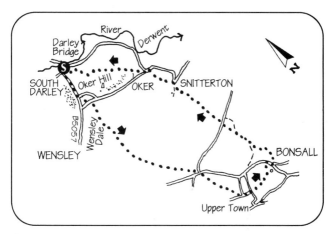

A faint way slants across to the next corner then up more open pasture to another corner stile. Head away to an old gateway just short of the end. Rise beneath an old spoil heap to a stile on the left, from where a good path runs through a colourful scrubby enclosure. At the end a steep climb leads to the remains of a wall. Look back to see Wensley beneath Stanton Moor, then up the Derwent to the Haddon and Chatsworth estates; Oker Hill is very much dwarfed now. Continue up with a line of grassy mounds to reach the top corner.

At this high level crossroads of paths take the stile ahead, not the corner one, and begin a splendid march through a dozen or so gap-stiles in quick succession, maintaining a straight line with the mast on Black Rocks above Cromford ahead. En route we pass near a

walled dewpond and across an enclosed pathway to emerge onto a road junction. Cross and resume from a stile opposite. Slanting up to a gap-stile in the rising wall keep on, bound for a barn several fields ahead, with the houses of Upper Town in front of the distant mast. Go left of the ramshackle barn to a stile, then off across the field centres bound for Upper Town. Straight on again, the faint path runs on to a corner stile by a gate onto another road junction.

Head straight along the road between the houses. On the right we pass a Post office/farm shop in an historic looking building, and a cottage with a 1775 datestone. **A T-junction with Bankside is reached by a former well. Virtually opposite take a short-lived lane, which quickly turns into a footway. Emerging into a field, keep straight on.** A super view is revealed, with Bonsall church spire appearing in the dip. **The path quickly becomes enclosed and remains largely so to descend steeply into Bonsall in front of the market cross.**

In the very brief spell where it breaks free from walls, an alternative path goes left through a stile, past a wall-corner then slants down to ultimately descend old steps in the field to emerge by houses onto High Street. Go right to the market cross, en route passing a superb old house with mullioned windows on the right, and the equally attractive Dower House on the left.

The hilly village of Bonsall - locally *Bonser* - has as its focal point a market cross on circular tiered steps. The shaft is dated 1671, and is complemented aesthetically and historically by the adjacent *King's Head* of 1677. Bonsall was a thriving lead mining community in the busy years of the 18th and 19th centuries and boasts some fine three-storey buildings, but today has been left in a no-man's land, tucked away with a sense of dereliction.

A tiny loop from the cross sends us right, past the pub. Just after the Baptist Chapel of 1824, turn up a path on the left, below a limestone scar to end up in the churchyard. St. James' church was restored in the 1860s but retains some 13th century features and a 450 year old spire. **Emerging at the top, go left on the road back down to the cross.**

Leave by a rough lane by the phone box immediately above the cross. This climbs steeply giving good views back over Bonsall. At the top take the footway left, running more tightly by brambles as it undulates along, rising again then on to a junction with a more

hollowed way. Turn up this to gain the brow of the hill. The latter section is a splendid, less enclosed green way. On the brow the track becomes enclosed by hedges: don't enter, but take a gap-stile to the left of the gate. Cross to a stile ahead and descend the wall-side onto a road, Salters Lane.

Bonsall

Cross straight over and slant right to a stile into Jughole Wood. The path drops down to a path fork at a stone trough on the sudden rim of a potentially dangerous ravine. Take the path straight ahead, running by the rim of this dark hole, and dropping down to spoil heaps beneath it. Here is the dark, quarried entrance: adventurous types who don't mind getting dirty have ventured in to climb back out of the hole through the gap below, emerging at the upper, less despoiled section already passed.

The path drops left of the spoil heaps and down the old mining enclosure, passing a ruinous kiln, a manhole cover hiding a sinister angled shaft, and also a capped shaft. Ignore any other branches and

77

go to a stile at the very bottom. **Drop straight down to Leawood Farm, passing through a couple of gates en route. Joining the track, keep right of the buildings and down the short drive onto a back road.** This last stage gives a glimpse through the trees to Snitterton Hall, a twin gabled manor house dating from around 1630, and featuring mullioned and transomed windows.

Go right down the road to a junction with the through road in the hamlet of Snitterton. On the verge outside Yew Tree Cottage is a stone inscribed *The Bull Ring Snitterton 22ft.* **Take a snicket on the left between houses into the field. Advance to a gate/stile, where a footpath sign indicates a fork.** Look over to the right to discern the grassy banks of a former moat. **With Oker sheltering beneath Oker Hill, head straight on, crossing a wooden farm bridge and up the fieldside to emerge onto a road on the edge of Oker.** This rather select hamlet has a former Wesleyan Methodist Chapel of 1832. **Go left and then quickly right on Aston Lane.** If desired, this will lead directly back to Darley Bridge.

The main way turns quickly off at a stile on the left. Slant up to the field top were a path enters the trees, rising through undergrowth to emerge onto a rough track. Turn right on here. Just above is the bracken flanked ridge of colourful Oker Hill, its crest at 633ft/193m being of very modest proportions, but serving as a fine local landmark and viewpoint.

The main way turns right along the track, becoming fainter as it rises past a roofless barn to the brow. Here we are greeted by big views up the Derwent Valley. **Keep straight on, dropping gently to enter an area of scrub. As it becomes denser the path forks at an old gateway: one goes straight on by a line of well aligned hawthorns, ours branches right to slant out of the trees. Keep straight on across to a stile, down a hollow and bear left along the field bottom to arrive at a lone house.**

Head out on its drive, briefly, then take a stile on the right and descend the fieldside. Across the tiny stream cross the level field to the nearest corner, and take a stile on the left. An alternative path keeps straight on to the far corner to join Oker Lane to finish. **The left branch runs on alongside an archery club (Derwent Bowmen): keep straight on in the corner to emerge, conveniently, into the pub car park and garden.**

18

MATLOCK DALE

START *Matlock Bath*   *Grid ref. SK 297584*

DISTANCE *3 miles*

ORDNANCE SURVEY MAPS
1:50,000
Landranger 119 - Buxton, Matlock & Dove Dale
1:25,000
Outdoor Leisure 24 - Peak District, White Peak

ACCESS *Start from Matlock Bath station (Derby-Matlock line), over the river from the A6: large car park. Buses from surrounding towns.*

Though outside the National Park, the natural attractions of Matlock Dale demand inclusion in these pages. Don't be fooled by the mileage, ample time should be allowed for some hilly walking and copious features of interest.

❺   Matlock is a busy little town comprising of a number of related settlements, some of which have been fully absorbed into the whole. Joined on to the south is Matlock Bath, in the heart of Matlock Dale, a deep limestone ravine through which the Derwent has cut. While Matlock has the shops, it is Matlock Bath that draws the tourists. This began late in the 17th century with the discovery of hot springs, whose potential medicinal properties prompted the creation of a spa town.

The boom years of the 19th century were amplified by the Victorians' delight at the scenery. The spa spread north from the dale's cramped confines to Matlock Bank, where the foremost hydropathic establishment (hydro) was built by John Smedley, a mill-owner: this survives as the County Council offices. Another claim to fame was the world's steepest cable tramway, which scaled Matlock Bank Road for a long half-mile at a gradient of 1 in 5½. Opened in 1891, it closed in 1927.

Matlock Bath's modern attractions include the Peak District Mining Museum alongside the Tourist Information Centre at the Pavilion, housing some major exhibits saved from the area's hectic lead mining times. Caves feature strongly in the Heights of Abraham's appeal, their cable cars drifting above the valley being an enticing advertisement. An aquarium and amusement arcades add a surreal touch to somewhere that couldn't be much further from the seaside.

Matlock Bath is penultimate station on the Derby to Matlock line, and its previously declining buildings, which date from 1849, are now occupied by Derbyshire Wildlife Trust as the Whistlestop Countryside Centre. It features an exhibition, video show, gifts and crafts.

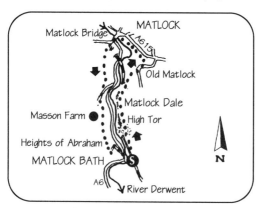

Immediately on embarking on this walk, High Tor rises ahead, a limestone crag surrounded in trees that will soon be much better seen. **Cross the single track line at the station and go left on a parallel pathway to the entrance to the cable cars. The footpath entrance to High Tor is right alongside.** The High Tor grounds are owned by the district council, having been laid out in Victorian times as pleasure grounds and romantic woodland walks. Visitors are requested to keep to waymarked paths, much of this being for their own safety as there are some alarming drops to the valley!

The path splits into numerous ways, all aiming for the top of High Tor. Keep to the left zigzags, all on good paths, to climb steeply through the trees. A sudden viewpoint overlooks Matlock Bath, with cable cars gliding up to the Heights of Abraham. **Gaining parity with**

an access road, the entrance to a limestone rift appears on the right. Fern Cave is well worthy of exploration, a 400ft long cleft that runs narrower and deeper as progress is made. There is escape at the end, out into the open, with the road just to the right. Better to return the same way though, forking right almost at the end to get back onto the path. **The summit is only a little further over more open ground.**

A seat and iron post occupy a rocky knoll, but the drop below is alarming, be warned. Not unexpectedly this is a prized viewpoint for the Matlock scene. The 350ft drop to the river includes High Tor's 150ft rockface, which offers dozens of top grade routes and a good chance of seeing some action on warm days. Prominent on the hilltop behind is Riber Castle, built by that man Smedley again in 1868. Destined to be little more than a folly, its gaunt shell currently looks over a rare breeds and endangered species park.

An optional extra on High Tor is the 'Giddy Edge Path', which traverses the rock face in dramatic fashion, reminiscent of something encountered on continental mountain trails. It starts just a few yards north of the summit, where a path doubles back to the left. Signs warn of its unsuitability for children and nervous types, for on this little adventure, the verticality is *Profound*. There is only one route, and the path soon re-emerges on the ascent path, so it's another five minutes back to the top.

Heading north proper, the path drops down to a crossroads, with a blocked cave on the right, a shelter seat on the left and a shack that served as a cafe just ahead. Bear left on the broad path descending the side of a recreation field, soon returning to the edge top to leave High Tor in far more leisurely mode than it was gained. Known as Arkwright's Grand Walk, the path was made by a direct descendant of Sir Richard Arkwright, pioneer of the Industrial Revolution (see WALK 19). Before the first viewing station be sure to look back to appreciate the awesome profile of High Tor. Continuing, the railway is seen emerging from the tunnel beneath us for its last half-mile to Matlock, which is itself outspread ahead.

The broad path runs unfailingly down above diminishing crags to join the end of a short lane. Go right on this to a road, then left down to St. Giles' parish church. A 1681 datestone adorns a lovely old house just before it. **Beyond the church a steep bank (Stoney Way) drops down, go left at the bottom on a streamside road. Keep left on**

a footway through the park, passing between pleasure grounds and a miniature railway along the riverbank to reach Matlock Bridge in the heart of the main town. Passing a footbridge, note the alarmingly high watermark in the flood of 9th December 1965.

Cross at the lights and go left over the bridge. On the right is the railway station, and alongside Peak Rail, who operate steam trains on a section of the former Midland Railway line north of this cul-de-sac. Plans are afoot to extend the line, with the ambitious aim of re-instating the full track to Buxton: the implications of a return of trains to tranquil Chee Dale are certainly thought-provoking!

High Tor, Matlock Dale

Continue straight on up the side road (Snitterton Road), but leave quickly by a waymarked branch left up a short drive to Bridge Farm, passing high above the railway. Continue up past the front of the house to a stile into a field. Climb this steep field but before the top take a branch left. Open views look to Riber Castle, and more impressively the sheer wall of the nearer High Tor.

Traces of kerbing are evident on this old pathway as it runs on through the fields to a corner stile. Go left along the wallside, contouring round the slope when the wall drops away. Around the corner the wall is rejoined, leading into some increasingly wooded country beneath Shining Cliff to emerge onto a drive.

Head up the drive, passing beneath the mysterious looking chapel of St. John, which celebrates its centenary as this book is published. At the entrance to Cliff House at the top, bear left on a firm track along the top of the wood. The right branch, incidentally, misleadingly lures the unwary into the idea they can reach the Heights of Abraham, when all you can actually do is peer through the trees like a second-class citizen!

The drive curves away, and when it swings up out of the trees to Masson Farm, keep left again, now on a footpath along the wood top. This runs pleasantly and undulatingly along, passing beneath a small crag and gradually rising a little to enter denser woodland in the private grounds of the Heights of Abraham. Named after the famous victory by General Wolfe in Quebec in 1759, this is now a large-scale tourist operation centred upon cable cars, caverns and scenic splendour. Fee-paying punters can be taken round the Rutland and Masson Caverns (once worked as lead mines), visit the hilltop Victoria Tower built in 1844 to draw visitors to the area, and generally amble around the labyrinthine path network.

For the most part the public path is enclosed by fencing to keep us riff-raff out! Crossing a curious bridge over a surfaced pathway within the grounds, it continues on and down to emerge onto the narrow Upperwood Road. Go left, and stay on the major road which quickly turns to drop down into Matlock Bath as Holme Road. The station is straight across the road. Further delights of Matlock Bath await here - two pubs 'on tap', and along to the right cafes, shops and of course the river.

19

BLACK ROCKS

START Cromford   *Grid ref. SK 299570*

DISTANCE 5 miles

ORDNANCE SURVEY MAPS
1:50,000
Landranger 119 - Buxton, Matlock & Dove Dale
1:25,000
Outdoor Leisure 24 - Peak District, White Peak

ACCESS Start from Cromford Wharf car park just off the A6 east of
Cromford village. Numerous bus services including Matlock, Crich,
Wirksworth, Chesterfield and Derby, and only five minutes from
Cromford station on the Derby-Matlock line.

An absorbing walk in a cradle of the Industrial Revolution, though
nature provides its own highlights. Richard Arkwright (knighted in
1786) was the man behind the development of Cromford, a remarkable entrepreneur who made Cromford what it is today.

🅢 Cromford Wharf marks the northern terminus of the Cromford
Canal. Opened in 1793, it ran 14½ miles to join the Erewash Canal,
thus linking to Derby and the Trent. Horse-drawn boats carried cotton,
textiles and anything that was being quarried or mined: limestone
predominantly but also coal, lead, iron and gritstone. It closed to
through traffic in 1900 following a tunnel collapse, and fully closed
in 1944. The old wharf itself has been undergoing restoration, and
there are toilets and sometimes refreshments available.

From the car park entrance turn right to take a look at the bridge.
Fifteenth century Cromford Bridge is a majestic span with contrasting
pointed and rounded arches on opposing sides. Alongside are the
scant remains of an equally old chapel, and an 18th century fishing

pavilion of humble stature bearing the Latin PISCATORIBUS SACRUM. **Return a few yards and turn into the drive by the church.** Arkwright is remembered in the church he began, though St. Mary's was not completed until after his death in 1792, and has since been restored.

The drive runs on past the church, upstream in the company of the Derwent to join the A6. Though in common use, this old carriageway is not a right of way: an emergency alternative would be the short road walk past Cromford Mill. The carriageway enjoys the river as a fine foreground to the large house of Willersley Castle, another Arkwright inspiration now owned by the Methodist church. In addition, we pass beneath the limestone crag of Scarthin Rock, a popular 130ft climbing rock that contrasts strongly with the Black Rocks to come.

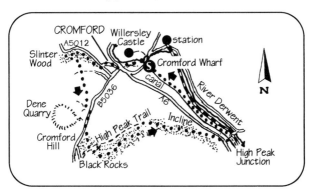

Cromford Mill was the site of the world's first successful water powered cotton spinning mill, established by Arkwright in 1771. Much of the original mill was destroyed by fire in 1930, though 150 years earlier it was also the first to have steam power. Today the mill is open to visitors, with a tour available as well as a shop and cafe.

At the main road go left to a small cafe by the lights, and cross to Cromford market place. Numerous shops are spread about, as well as the *Boat Inn* and the elegant Georgian *Greyhound Inn*, built to accommodate visitors to the mill. **Turn sharp right up a narrow one-way road known as Scarthin, at the end dropping onto the A5012.** En route we pass a millpond beyond which the Black Rocks stand high on the wooded hillside (the old cornmill still has its waterwheel in working order); and Scarthin Books where refreshments are on offer.

Cross the main road and along a short roadway. A path climbs away, but at the first chance, after an allotment, take a branch right into trees. Passing beneath an old quarry the path runs upstream above a millpond into Slinter Wood. After a large quarry entrance across the main road, a waymark sends a path doubling back left. It climbs steeply through trees to a breach in the craggy wall at the top. A short branch left invites a cautious gaze out from an airy stance over the wooded valley and busy road to appreciate the interior of the quarry.

Just through the rocks, a fence-stile admits into a field. The view ahead opens out to reveal the mast on Bole Hill above the Black Rocks, and also down the Derwent Valley to the prominent hilltop monument above Crich. Go right, along the tree line and mineshaft line, passing through a gateway as the way starts to drop markedly. Cross another gateway then drop down to a kissing-gate onto the enclosed old pathway of Alabaster Lane. Cross straight over to enter Derbyshire Wildlife Trust's Rose End Meadows.

A path heads over the brow and along the pasture top. Advance on through several stiles and past a dewpond on this clear path. At the end it drops down to leave the reserve, with the large Dene Quarry and upper Cromford ahead. The path descends steeply to the end of a rough road, along it then left to join the B5036 on Cromford Hill.

Cross and turn uphill for a few minutes on a footway, passing the quarry entrance and leaving the houses behind. With Black Rocks looming above, leave the road at a footpath sign pointing along a private looking drive just short of the woods. This is quickly vacated by veering left up an enclosed track, rising to emerge at the foot of the trees beneath a spoil heap. The white spoil is a result of the extraction of calcite from former lead workings.

Take the right branch which climbs as a good path through Dimons Dale to meet the High Peak Trail. The Black Rocks are directly above, but it may be deemed worth detouring right for a few yards to the Black Rocks Information Centre. The Black Rocks area is managed by Forest Enterprise and the county council. A few yards from the centre is the (covered!) 400ft shaft of Cromford Moor Mine.

The High Peak Trail makes use of the former Cromford & High Peak Railway, built to link the Cromford Canal with the Peak Forest Canal at Whaley Bridge, beyond Buxton. It became fully operational in 1831 with horse-drawn waggons linking nine inclines, one of which we shall soon encounter. Within a dozen years steam locomotives largely replaced the horses. For more than 20 years a passenger service also operated: a fatal accident in 1877 brought that venture to a premature end. All the little stations were called wharves to complement the canal system: indeed, originally the entire route was optimistically mooted as a canal!

Though the western part of the line closed a century ago, that to Parsley Hay on the Ashbourne-Buxton line survived into the 1960s, the last section closing in 1967. For many of its declining years it was in the hands of the London & North Western Railway, who already ran the other line. Derbyshire County Council and the National Park took up the challenge of converting 17½ miles to leisure use, the entire route to just short of Buxton being passable to bridleway users.

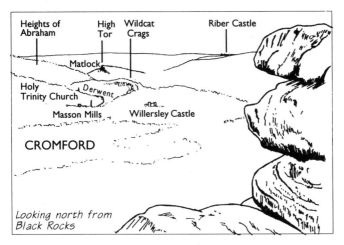

Heights of Abraham   High Tor   Wildcat Crags   Riber Castle

Matlock

Holy Trinity Church   Derwent

Masson Mills   Willersley Castle

CROMFORD

Looking north from Black Rocks

One might simply turn left along the trail and get on with it, but the Black Rocks await: take the main path climbing to the rocks. The Black Rocks of Cromford (Sunday name) is an impressive rounded gritstone outcrop popular with climbers for more than a century and, fittingly, with around a hundred recorded routes on offer: mere mortals can also gain the top from the back. Not surprisingly it is a splendid viewpoint looking up the Derwent Valley, though the scale of Dene Quarry puts the earlier enterprise well in the shade! The Matlock Bath environs include the features illustrated above: the red-brick Masson Mills (on the roadside between Cromford and Matlock Bath) was another major Arkwright venture.

Again one can simply return to the trail and head off, but parts of forest trails can be used to add further variety. **Rising behind the rocks are waymarked blue and green trails. Take the main path rising away, soon turning into the woods beneath a well colonised old quarry. They then turn again to rise up the far side of the quarry. When the blue one climbs up to its rim, the green bears left into the trees.**

Remain on the green route, passing a tract of open country to meet the blue again at a junction. Now advance straight on the blue one, pleasantly along to a T-junction near the edge of the wood. Go left, soon narrowing to reach a well defined edge, where it drops quickly to rejoin the High Peak Trail at the top of Sheep Pasture Incline.

More excellent views are earned from a perfect platform, looking out over Matlock Dale with features much the same as from the Black Rocks. The abandoned track-side building is the shell of the Sheep Pasture engine house. Opened in 1838 it housed a stationery steam winding engine which hauled waggons up the incline from the canal wharf. Its maximum gradient was 1 in 8, and all but one of its fellow inclines were also worked by these engines. The only remaining engine of its type is preserved at Middleton Top Visitor Centre, a mile or two distant from here.

From the engine house head down the long incline, initially through a rock cutting and all the way through fine woodland. At the bottom it passes under the A6 to arrive at High Peak Junction. The black hole on the right just before the road tunnel was a catchpit, built as its name suggests to halt runaway waggons on the incline (indeed, the remains of one are still inside!).

High Peak Junction was the goods wharf for the canal. Today it houses a visitor centre (in summer and on winter weekends), shop, toilets, refreshments and a ranger's office. It claims the oldest surviving railway workshops in the world, which visitors can pay to look round. Just back along the canal is the mid-19th century Leawood pumphouse with its imposing chimney, built to take water from the Derwent to the canal in times of shortage. On occasions in summer a steam engine operates here.

Cross the bridge and turn left on the towpath. This leads unerringly back, over a long mile, to Cromford Wharf. Initially wooded as it parallels railway and river, it later opens out, passing beneath a stone arched bridge and above sports fields to return to the start.

BRASSINGTON

START Carsington   Grid ref. SK 249528

DISTANCE 7½ miles

ORDNANCE SURVEY MAPS
1:50,000
Landranger 119 - Buxton, Matlock & Dove Dale
1:25,000
Outdoor Leisure 24 - Peak District, White Peak

ACCESS Start from Severn-Trent Water's Sheepwash car park at Carsington Water, on the B5035 Wirksworth-Ashbourne road near Carsington village. Served by infrequent Ashbourne-Matlock buses.

From the springboard of Carsington Reservoir this smashing walk takes in old lead mining country, evidence now largely restricted to grassy mounds in the fields; two pleasant villages and two contrasting rocky outcrops further combine with a section of the High Peak Trail to make a richly varied outing. Entirely outside the National Park, this walk through dolomitic limestone country is very much on a par with its gritstone counterpart around Harthill Moor, a little further north.

S Opened by Her Majesty the Queen in 1992, Carsington claims the 20th century's last major reservoir, though it was not without controversial engineering 'hiccups' during its attempted construction in the 1980s. Further round the western shore a large visitor centre boasts exhibition, shop, restaurant, refreshments, first aid, toilets and play area. It is a haven for wildfowl and migrant birds in what was once the valley of Scow Brook. Fly fishing and bird hides allow you either to hunt or admire God's creatures, while cyclists can, like walkers, enjoy a circuit of the reservoir. Watersports also feature strongly of course, while a wide range of organised events also take place throughout the year.

Return towards the car park entrance, and after the information boards take a signed footpath off to the right through scattered trees. It runs on a fence side with views ahead of Carsington Pasture. At a fork keep right with the fence as the path winds around a feeder of the reservoir to reach a stile onto the B5035. Cross straight over and up a path that becomes enclosed, broadening into a lane to emerge into Carsington. Go left, possibly with a diversion up a short path onto the higher road.

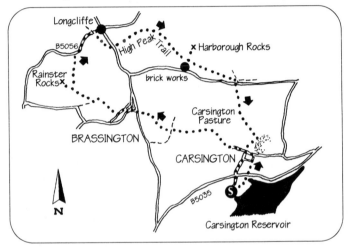

Carsington is a very small, former lead mining community, now a peaceful backwater known only for the name it gave the new reservoir. In addition to St. Margaret's tiny church dating from 1648, there is a pub, the distinguished three-storey *Miners Arms*; a cross shaft on the triangular green; and a number of handsome cottages with gardens to match.

Go left on the street to where the road swings left out of the village. Here keep straight on the no through road, emerging at the end as a track into Carsington Pasture. Head off on this good grassy way, curving round the foot of the pasture. In the field ahead are distinct evidences of medieval ridge and furrow ploughing. There are also good views down over the reservoir. Stay with the wall as the track swings round to a combination of gates, stile and cattle-grid where a fence meets it.

Across, branch up to the right on a well defined groove, slanting above a line of mineshafts to a crumbling wall. A stile survives to point the way on to the next decaying wall, on the very brow. Just to our left are limestone boulders in the trees, while over to the right in the vicinity of the abandoned Wester Head Mines, the slopes display a bizarre arrangement of large upright boulders resembling a Tibetan village: this odd dolomitic limestone is the first of numerous more impressive examples to come. **Drop down the field to a stile, and across to one onto a green lane.**

Cross straight over and up an old quarry track, branching left of it to curve round the edge of the knoll, revealing Brassington village spread across the opposite slope. The path curves down a colourful old mining pasture of scrub and occasional outcrops. Towards the bottom slant down through a stile before joining the base wall. Go right to a stile in it, then down the wallside. A stile part-way down sends the way across a couple more fields to a corner stile, emerging via the side of a garden onto the road in Brassington.

Brassington is an attractive village founded on the busy lead mining times, at their peak in the 18th century. Some of its mellow limestone houses date back to the start of this period. Just down to the left is the architecturally intriguing Tudor House, with a 1615 datestone and mullioned and transomed windows. **Cross at this junction and turn up the road opposite, to the *Miners Arms*.** Like Carsington, it leaves little doubt about its history. St. James' church sits importantly just above, featuring a Norman tower and work from most subsequent centuries up to the restoration of 1881.

Either enter the churchyard or go left on the road in front. Just along the lane are a second pub, *Ye Olde Gate Inne*, and a Post office/shop: the latter was once a tollhouse, hence the pub name. Two other attractive houses bear 1774 and 1737 datestones. **A path runs up the far side of the churchyard, climbing to a narrow back road.**

Go left, passing a redundant Primitive Methodist Chapel. As the road starts to drop take a stile on the right, and a path curves around the pasture, rising towards the end to a stile. Slant up the larger pasture, and across to a gate/stile at the far end, with a first glimpse of Rainster Rocks ahead. Entering the head of a green lane, go left a short way to find a stile on the right. Another vast colourful pasture is entered, with Rainster Rocks upstanding directly across a hollow.

Slant down through the scrub, crossing a very faint green bridleway and passing a miniature gnarled outcrop to a stile in the intervening wall. Head for the rocks, passing a guidepost at a footpath crossroads to which we shall return. For now though, rise up to the rocks. Though competently defended by a dense skirt of scrub, this is worth penetrating to gain the rocks.

The main face points southwards, some of its dolomite limestone being as gnarled as the scrub. The crest can be gained by the near side or a simple chimney just past the main face. The place engenders a sense of discovery, almost as though no-one had been here before. In truth, dozens of short rock climbs have been recorded, largely in the lower grades by virtue of inviting holds not accorded to 'normal' limestone!

Rainster Rocks

Dropping back to the path crossroads, bear left to a gateway at the top, just past which a bridleway joins in at a bridle-gate (not quite as the map suggests). This continues up the wallside, joining a firmer track by some barns to lead out onto the B5056. Turn right for a few minutes up to the brow, passing beneath more shapely outcrops. Turn the corner with caution to find the High Peak Trail just ahead.

Pass under the bridge to the hamlet of Longcliffe, and before the first house a stile on the right puts us onto the trail at the old station. Turn left for a good stride of almost two miles.

En route we have a sharp bend to escape unsightly works on the left. Emerging from a second, longer rock cutting, Harborough Rocks appear on the slopes ahead. The long straight sections, sharp curves and steep inclines (not seen on this walk) of this line are an irregular railway feature, owing their existence to a canal engineer. For more on the railway and the trail, please refer to WALK 19.

At the end of the large brickworks a stile on the left sends an optional path up to explore the rocks: rise to another stile above to gain the environs of the rocks. Harborough Rocks (illustrated on page 1) are a fine array of upright boulders strewn across the hillside, in strong contrast to the confined characteristics of our previous highlight. The rock itself is typical of the locality, being fine examples of rough, weathered dolomitic limestone. Easily found is a cave that has yielded evidence of occupation through numerous ages. Also worth seeking is the rock fashioned into a chair, complete with the date 1757. An Ordnance Survey column at 1243ft/379m crowns the grouping, and offers a magnificent all-round panorama.

The trail runs on a further dead straight half-mile to the next footpath branch, yards short of a road. From a stile on the right go down the fieldside to a road, straight over and down into the vast Carsington Pasture, again. Over to the left the forlorn sight of a windmill lacking sails and roof languishes in the field. The way simply heads down the wallside, up to the brow and bears left with the wall. Ahead, the reservoir returns to view, while the day's last odd rock formation over the wall is a modest effort known as the King's Chair.

Approaching the wood at the end turn down to the right, slanting steeply down towards the village which appears in bird's-eye fashion. En route, keep a wary eye on the numerous circular pits containing capped shafts: Carsington Pasture is renowned for the profusion of such holes (over 200), and not all are guaranteed safe! Aim for the solitary house at the base of the pasture, and a small gate gives access to a pathway dropping down onto a narrow lane and thence the road in the village. Either return through the village, or more directly by following the road straight out and down to the main road, across which is the car park entrance.

LOG OF THE WALKS

WALK	DATE	NOTES
1		
2		
3		
4		
5		
6		
7		
8		
9		
10		
11		
12		
13		
14		
15		
16		
17		
18		
19		
20		

INDEX

Principal features: walk number refers

THE PEAK DISTRICT

Explore on foot Britain's most popular National Park with a comprehensive set of 5 guidebooks. Each contains 20 walks.

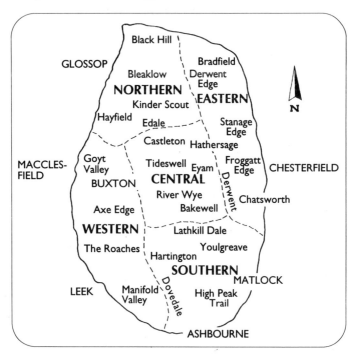

•**NORTHERN PEAK**   ISBN 1 870141 48 2
  Edale/Kinder Scout/Longdendale/Bleaklow/Hayfield/Mam Tor
•**EASTERN PEAK**   ISBN 1 870141 50 4
  Derwent Valley/Baslow/Eastern Edges/Chatsworth/Ladybower
•**CENTRAL PEAK**   ISBN 1 870141 51 2
  Bakewell/Wye Dale/Eyam/Monsal Dale/Tideswell/Miller's Dale
•**SOUTHERN PEAK**   ISBN 1 870141 52 0
  Dovedale/High Peak Trail/Lathkill Dale/Matlock/Tissington Trail
•**WESTERN PEAK**   ISBN 1 870141 54 7
  Buxton/The Roaches/Goyt Valley/Manifold Valley/Shutlingsloe